**Her Aching Heart**, **Two Marias** and **Wicked**

'Bryony Lavery has finally come out. After years in the closet, she has admitted to a consuming passion for romantic fiction. **Her Aching Heart** celebrates this and gives it all a neat contemporary twist. If it's torn fichus and pounding hearts you're after, you'll not be disappointed.'

Betty Caplan, *Guardian*

Set in Andalucía, Spain, the lyrical and poignant **Two Marias** explores family identity, love, death and faith.

**Wicked**: 'When Bailey the impresario in lilac silk and a black plastic coif produces his female freaks from boxes for the audience's entertainment, he unleashes a string of characters, uproarious cabaret-style comedy, magic and illusion. A celebration of female survival.'

Barbara Norden, *City Limits*

**Bryony Lavery**'s plays include: **Helen and Her Friends** (1978); **Bag** (1979); **Family Album** (1980); **Missing** (1981); **Hot Time** (1984); **Calamity** (1984); **Origin of the Species** (1984); **Witchcraze** (1985); **The Headless Body** (1987); **Puppet States** (1988); **Kitchen Matters** (1990) and **Flight** (1991). She was Resident Playwright at the Unicorn Theatre for Children, 1986–87 and her work for children includes: **The Zulu Hut Club** (1983); **Sore Points** (1986); **Madagascar** (1987) and **The Dragon Wakes** (1988). Her cabaret work includes: **Female Trouble** (1981); **More Female Trouble** (1982); **The Wandsworth Warmers** (1984) and **The Wandsworth Warmers Unbridled Passion** (1986). Bryony was Artistic Director for Gay Sweatshop, 1989–1991 and she is currently a Tutor in Playwriting at Birmingham University.

**Methuen New Theatrescripts** series offers frontline intelligence of the most original and exciting work from the fringe:

*Authors in the same series*

Mike Alfreds &
  Michelene Wandor
Iraj Jannatie Ataie
Harwant S Bains
Sebastian Barry
Aphra Behn
Edward Bond
Howard Brenton
Richard Cameron
Sarah Daniels
Nick Darke
Nick Dear
Harvey Fierstein
Peter Gibbs
Paul Godfrey
André Gregory
Robert Holman
Kevin Hood
Debbie Horsfield
Tunde Ikoli
Terry Johnson
Charlotte Keatley
Manfred Karge
Barrie Keeffe
Thomas Kilroy

David Lan
Deborah Levy
Kate Lock
Stephen Lowe
Doug Lucie
David Mamet
Marlane Meyer
Anthony Minghella
Adrian Mitchell
Gregory Motton
Tom Murphy
Louise Page
Christina Reid
Philip Ridley
Rob Ritchie
David Rudkin
Jeremy Sams
Wallace Shawn
Jack Shepherd
David Spencer
C P Taylor
Peter Whelan
Michael Wilcox
Rod Wooden
Nicholas Wright

# Her Aching Heart
# Wicked
# Two Marias

*Bryony Lavery*

Methuen Drama

**A Methuen New Theatrescript**

This collection first published in Great Britain in 1991 by
Methuen Drama, Michelin House, 81 Fulham Road, London SW3 6RB
and distributed in the United States of America by HEB Inc.,
361 Hanover Street, Portsmouth, New Hampshire, NH 03801 3959

A CIP catalogue record for this book is available
from the British Library.

ISBN 0-413-66060-5

The photograph on the front cover shows Nicola Kathrens (left) as
Lady Harriet Helstone and Sarah Kevney as Molly Penhallow from the
Women's Theatre Group touring production of *Her Aching Heart*.
Photograph by Ute Klaphake.

Typeset in 9½/11pt Linotron Baskerville by Wilmaset, Birkenhead, Wirral
Printed and bound in Great Britain by Cox & Wyman Ltd, Reading

**Caution**

## Introduction

The three plays included in this volume were all commissioned by small, brave theatre companies who continue – despite parsimonious funding, insufficient personnel, drafty, poky office space, truculent, decrepit Mercedes vans and far-flung theatre venues cannily situated up five flights of stairs – to produce new, exciting theatre pieces for the delectation of audiences from Newcastle to the Isle of Wight.

**Her Aching Heart**, for the Women's Theatre Group, started off with a brief to write 'a two-hander exploring sexuality and gender'. Hmmm – catchy. Claire Grove (the director) and I felt somewhat mournful and worthy about the project, until we discovered a mutual addiction to romantic fiction. We decided, courageously, to Come Out. Luckily, I had spent my girlish teens alternately swotting for Latin, English and History 'A' levels and bunking off to read Georgette Heyer and Daphne du Maurier. Admirers of the English education system will discover in the text a cornucopia of romantic gush, at least five non-adjacent historical periods . . . and five words of Latin.

**Two Marias**, for Theatre Centre, was written for audiences of seventeen-year-old schoolgirls. Since I had waved goodbye to that age some aeons ago, the brief was difficult until I remembered reading, in a Sunday paper, the story of Maria del Amor and Maria del Morte. I was suffering grief over the death of a friend, Philip Tyler, and this play, which recalls the dead, helped me to understand it in some measure. The play was performed in school halls with the audience on four sides of a Spanish courtyard. The seventeen-year-old girls found it a rattling good story. The teachers supervising them were invariably reduced to tears. It is, of course, a play for those attacked by death.

**Wicked**, for Clean Break, was written to be performed in prisons by women ex-offenders. The title of the play is my uncomplicated response to the prison system – it is grim, frightening, damaging, soul-destroying, evil . . . wicked. The women subjected to prison possess extraordinary courage and outrageous senses of humour. The play is a fiction in which the women break out of their locked-up places and stay free. The facts are horribly different.

Bryony Lavery, August 1991

# Her Aching Heart

**Her Aching Heart** was first performed by the Women's Theatre Group at the Oval House, London on 23 May 1990 with the following cast:

**Harriet**
**Lady Harriet Helstone**      Nicola Kathrens
**Granny**
**Joshua**

**Molly**
**Molly Penhallow**            Sarah Kevney
**Betsy**
**Lord Rothermere**

*Directed by* Claire Grove
*Designed by* Amanda Fisk
*Music written by* Juliet Hill
*Music arranged by* Juliet Hill, Janette Mason and Ros Mason
*Lighting by* Lizz Poulter

# Act One

## A Broken-Hearted Woman Sings

*There is a woman. Her name is* **Harriet**. *She is broken-hearted. She sings.*

*Song: Uninvited*

**Harriet**
After too many cigarettes
After too much gin
When I think 'I'll go to bed'
That's when you come in
You creep into my mind
And say 'Hello'
Babe . . you weren't invited
Please will you go?

I didn't invite you
Didn't ask you my dear
Babe . . you're unwelcome
So why are you here?

After I've played too many tracks
After too much sound
When I think 'that's quite enough'
That's when you call round
You steal into my heart
And say 'Hello'
Babe . . you weren't invited
Please will you go?

I didn't invite you
Thought I'd made it clear
Babe . . . you're unwelcome
So why are you here?

After I've picked out a good book
After thumbing through
When I think 'bedtime reading'

The words all say 'you'
You crawl into my head
And say 'Hello'
Babe . . . you weren't invited
Please will you go?

I didn't invite you
Thought I'd made it clear
Babe . . . you're unwelcome
So why are you here?

*She sighs, mooches around, picks up a book, looks at the cover.*

**Harriet** (*reads*) 'Her Aching Heart.' (*She laughs wrily.*) 'A lesbian historical romance.' (*She sighs, opens the book, reads.*) 'Last night I dreamt I went to Helstone Hall again. It seemed to me I stood before the intricately-wrought iron gate leading to the densely-wooded drive, and for a while I could not enter for the way was barred to me.' (*She laughs wrily, stands up, collects what she needs to, reads.*) 'There was a lock and chain keeping shut the gate.'

*Reading still, she exits. As she does, the book itself opens up and we are inside it.*

## Chapter One: A Nun Has A Nightmare

*A woman enters, dressed in a shift. Her heart is aching. Anguish clouds her sweet eyes.*

**Molly** Last night I dreamt I went to Helstone Hall again. It seemed to me I stood before the intricately-wrought iron gate leading to the densely-wooded drive, and for a while I could not enter for the way was barred to me. There was a lock and chain keeping shut the gate. I called in my dream to the lodge-keeper . . crusty, kindly Samuel, 'Helloooo! Let me by!' But no answer came and peering through the rusted rococo I saw that Samuel's cheery cottage was empty. No smoke curled from the chimney. No smell of baking bread issued from the gaping door. No comfort met me.

Then, like all dreamers, I was possessed of a sudden with
supernatural powers . . . and I passed like a spirit through the
gate and was racing, like a thing possessed, up the twisting drive.
Past the gnarled oaks choked with ivy. Past the rhododendron
bushes twisted and tortured. Past the bracken rank and wild.
And I stood before the mighty, looming presence of Helstone
Hall.

*She clutches at her heart.*

Oooooooh! Dear Watcher, it was EMPTY!!!!! The Great Lawn,
once smooth and green as a billiard table . . . was tossed and
torn with mole-mounds . . . The soaring grey-granite walls were
choked and poked with thrusting tendrils of ivy . . The mullioned
windows, once twinkling with bubbled bright glass, were broken,
dark . . like blinded eyes. Helstone Hall was an empty shell, just
as is now my breast where once beat my gentle heart.

*Her tears flow, like the River Dart, fast and furious. She picks up a black
garment, wipes her eyes upon it. She puts it on.*

Moonlight can play odd tricks upon the fancy . . for in my
dream, excitement rippled through my slight form . . and I could
swear the house was not empty . . but pulsed with life . . . .
Pungent woodsmoke puffed from the myriad chimney pots, warm
light from many-branched silver candlesticks streamed from the
windows and the warm night air carried the sound of human
voices.

*There is the sound of human voices.*

The wild and extravagant Helstones down from London with
their rakish friends . . . the rich and dissolute men, (*She puts on a
white close-fitting hood.*) the beautiful powdered women (*She puts on
a cross.*) and at the centre of that glittering throng rich and lovely
ardent and wilful the impetuous Lady Harriet Helstone. (*She puts
on a wimple.*) Harriet. (*With warm affection.*) Harriet. (*With lust.*)
Harriet. (*With longing.*) Harriet. (*With hatred.*) Harriet. (*With
emptiness.*) Harriet.

*She picks up a Bible and exits.*

## Chapter Two: A Lady Attends To Her Toilet

*The sound of human voices continues. A woman enters in historical underwear. She is beautiful, wild, wilful and wearily discontented.*

**Harriet** Oh how *weary* I am of our rakish friends! How tired I am of rich and dissolute men! How fatigued I am with beautiful and powdered women! Small wonder I am ardent and wilful! Small wonder London society is agog with my outrageous pranks. Little wonder that a devil of discontent mars my otherwise lovely countenance!

*She stares at the devil of discontent reflected in her chevalier glass.*

What do these laughing grey eyes look for? What will warm these rose-petalled cheeks? What can quicken the lips of this generous mouth? I let Rothermere steal a kiss last night.

*She sighs discontentedly.*

Twas tiresome! Tralala . . . what care I if the servants talk, if Mama looks cross, if Papa threatens to take me still across his knee . . . even though I have put up my hair and been received in Polite Society!!! Where is Betsy? I want to get dressed!!!

*Rings a bell.*

Not here! . . . I'll beat the scamp! Very well . . . I'll dress myself! Ah . . . my riding habit!

*She puts it on.*

How well it fits my magnificent figure. I'll cut a dash in the field today! Ah . . . my boots! Polished with a secret concoction of boot-blacking and champagne known only to my father's gentleman! Ah . . . my hat! I'll set it at a rakish angle to show off its Parisienne millinery! There!

*She picks up a riding crop. Stares at herself in the glass.*

Harriet. Today's the hunt. Mount your black stallion Thunderer . . the one Papa says is too strong for a lady . . . (*She laughs.*) Call your dogs . . . Jasper! . . . Judas! . . . Julian! . . . Follow the fox! (*We hear the sounds of horses, dogs.*) Lose yourself in the hunt!!!

*A horn blows.* **Harriet** *exits.*

## Another Broken-Hearted Woman Sings A Song

**Molly** *comes on in modern dress. She is reading* Her Aching Heart

**Molly** 'And it seemed to me in my dream, that when I called her name I was no longer a votive nun dedicated to prayers, humility and chastity . . . and growing God's greenery in my beloved monastery garden . . . but was transported back in time . . . as can happen in dreams . . . to that day I first encountered . . . her . . . .'

*She sighs.*
*She mooches around.*
*She sings*

*Song: Heart Surgery*

**Molly**
Gave it up
Loving
Bad for my heart.
Gave it up
Feeling
Tore me apart.

Should have read the warning
'Loving can seriously damage your health'
But it's an addiction
And creeps up by stealth.

Well, doctor
You had my heart in your hand
That's why there's blood on your sleeve.
Well, doctor
The operation hurt me
But that's normal I believe

Gave it up
Loving
Bad for my heart.
Gave it up
Feeling
Tore me apart

Heart surgery
All for the best
Left me with just
This machine ticking away in my breast

*She sighs, mooches around, picks up the book again, reads.*

'Harriet. Her name spoke to my heart. Harriet!'

Harriet . . . . (*She finds a piece of cigarette packet in her pocket. She reads the telephone number on it.*)

'Harriet . . . 071 294 6033' Mmm . . . . Harriet.

*She exits as* **Harriet** *enters.*

**Harriet** (*in riding habit*) What a fresh, fine, sharp Cornish morning. I declare . . . it lifts my heart like a sparrow . . . tossing it in winged joy on gently-wafting currents of air! The trees rustle in the light wind! The sun streaks like a basset hound across the fields! The sea gallops like a thoroughbred mare pounding its shiny hooves upon the rocks along the shore! Oh what a day! Oh what a wind of hope blows through the echoing corridors of my breast! rattling at the knobs and knockers of the doors to my dry and dusty emotions! I shall flush some wild game from the hedgerows and chase it far this morn! To the Hunt!!!!!

*Hunting horns.*
*Hooves.*
*Hounds.*


## Chapter Three: Thorns

*A briar and bramble thicket on the wilder reaches of the Helstone estate. The nun enters . . . She is dressed as a young village maiden. She is unaware of this.*

**Molly** And it seemed to me, in my dream, that when I called her name . . . I was no longer a votive nun . . . I was again that simple, untried eighteen-year-old village maiden . . with that clear translucent skin.

*She puts her hand up to her face and is shocked to feel that it is clear and translucent.*

Aaaaaaah!!! Wearing my simple rough holland gown.

*She puts her hands to her breast and is shocked to feel that it is covered with simple rough holland material.*

Aaaaaaah!!!

*She looks down and sees how she is dressed.*

I was again picking blackberries in a briar and bramble thicket on the wilder reaches of the Helstone estate . .

*She sees the thorn bushes.*

Aaaaaaaaaaaaah!!!!! How strong the dream is! It is as if . . . . I could reach out . . and feel the prick of the thorn on my finger . .

*She reaches out and feels the prick of the thorn on her finger.*

Ooooooooow!!! It is as if . . . . . I could pick a blackberry . . . put it in my mouth . . . and taste its soft sweetness!

*She picks a blackberry . . puts it in her mouth . . . and tastes its soft sweetness. We hear the baying of hounds, the horn, the thundering of hooves. She is eighteen again.*

(*Suddenly alert.*) What was that? (*She listens.*) Why . . it's The Helstone Hunt! Coming this way! I must away before they catch me on their land!!! Rumour has it that the Helstones *thrash* common folk found on their demesne!

*Suddenly, a fox races on.*

A fox! Ah, poor hunted beast! I'll save you.

*She picks up the fox. It is quivering with fright.*

Oh, poor thing . . . you're quivering with fright! What can we do? I'll take you home to my poor but specklessly clean cottage . . Oh no . . . my gown is caught on the thorn bush! I'm trapped! Oh no!!!!

*The baying of hounds, the horn, the thundering of hooves reaches a crescendo. Offstage we hear . . .*

**Harriet** (*off*) Hold your horses! Hold them I say! Curb those hounds! Curb them I say! The fox has gone to ground in this dense copse of thorns!!! I'll dismount . . . here . . . hold Thunderer . . I'll beat a way through with my riding crop and flush out Wily Reynard!!! No no . . . I'll go on my own!

**Harriet** *enters, mud-splashed and glowing.*

Now, where are you . . you pointed snouted murderer of poultry? AaaaH!

*She stops short.*

God's Wounds! What have we here? A Trespasser. A Peasant by the look of that rough holland gown. But why all aquiver? Hare an' Hounds! She holds my fox!!!!

*She is understandably furious.*

Girl . . . peasant . . . underling . . you interrupt my hunt! Let go the fox!

**Molly** Madam . . . I will not.

**Harriet** You will not? Madam . . . come here to me!

**Molly** Madam I cannot.

**Harriet** You cannot? Madam . . I am Gentry . . . have you taken leave of your senses?

**Molly** Madam . . I have not.

**Harriet** Will not . . cannot . . . have not . . You are all nots! And so you will be if I tie you hand and foot and beat the nots out of you you will be knots indeed!!!

**Molly** Madam . . . I *will* not for all my life I have loved the creatures of the field and wood and they, responding, all come to me with broken wings, sore paws, dislocated ears . . . Madam . . . I *cannot* for I am trapped in this thorny spot by sharp briars. Madam . . . I *have* not for I know you will not kill this fox!

**Harriet** Why will I not kill the fox, you impudent girl?

**Molly** For within your breast, Madam, beats a woman's heart.

**Harriet** Wrong, Madam! I have no heart at all! Ask any man in London! I am the wilful Lady Harriet Helstone and I take what I want and the fox is mine!

**Molly** Lady Harriet Helstone . . . ?

**Harriet** Yes!

**Molly** . . . of Helstone Hall . . . ?

**Harriet** Yes!

**Molly** . . . of the hellraising Helstones . . . ?

**Harriet** Yes.

**Molly** Madam . . . let me go.

**Harriet** Madam I will.

**Harriet** *kneels to release* **Molly**'s *gown.*

**Molly** (*looking down in wondering surprise on* **Harriet**'s *elegant riding hat*) She releases me . . . .

**Harriet** (*looking down in wondering surprise on* **Molly**'s *shabby holland gown*) I release her . . . .

*They look into each other's countenances for what seems like an aeon.*

*At the same time, both shake their heads as if they are dismissing an almighty and unwelcome thought.*

**Harriet** I let you go . . . . But I will take the fox!

**Molly** No!!!

**Harriet** Yes!!!

**Molly** See how he quivers!!!

**Harriet** You both quiver!!!

*They do.*

**Molly** He with fright . . . I with passion!!!!!!!!!!!! Look into his eyes . . see how they roll in terror! Observe his sharp teeth rigid in a rictus of fear! See his proud tail bushy and upstanding with fright! Understand the determination which courses like *Fire* through every fibre of my being! You will not kill this fox!!!

**Harriet** And understand the wilfulness which storms like a *Tornado* through every fibre of *my* being! I will kill this fox!!!

**Molly** You *indescribable monster*!!!!

**Harriet** You *unconscionable upstart*!!! The fox goes with me!

**Molly** The fox stays!

*The fox takes an active interest in this exchange.*

**Harriet** I have a riding whip!

**Molly** I have sharp teeth. So does the fox!

**Harriet** I will beat you until you are black and blue!

**Molly** I will bite you until *you* are black and blue. And so will the fox.

**Harriet** I will beat you until your rough holland gown is as thin as silk!

**Molly** I will bite you until your magnificent riding habit hangs in tatters and rags! And so will the fox.

**Harriet** I will take you to my opulent bed and there on the fine satin sheets I will kiss your lips with such intention that I will kiss out your soul . . .

**Molly** I will take you to my truckle bed and there on the simple cotton sheet I will touch your body with such intention that I will bring forth your soul . . . .

**Harriet** What?

**Molly** What?

*Surely they both misheard.*

**Harriet** I misheard.

**Molly** I misheard. So did the fox. I am going to set down the fox . . . and you are going to let him escape . . .

**Harriet** Try it!

**Molly** I do. See. (*She sets down the fox.*) Run, Reynard. (*Oddly enough, it doesn't.*)

**Harriet** Run, Reynard. (*She hits it with her riding crop.*) Escape, fool!!!

*Sadly, this makes the fox run in the wrong direction . . . towards the hunt.*

**Molly** Oh yes!

**Harriet** Oh no!

*There is a baying of hounds, a thundering of hooves, a horn, excited cries.*

**Molly** Oh no!

**Harriet** No . . . . no . . . no . . no . . . NOOOOOOOO! (*She hurries off.*)

**Molly** No . . . oh . . no . . . please . . . no . . . no . . NOOOOOOOOOO!!!

*There is a bloodcurdling, fox-like scream.* **Molly** *collapses, weeping.*

**Harriet** *returns with her hands covered in blood.*

**Harriet** Too late. Poor Reynard. I . . . .

**Molly** Enough! (*She wipes away her tears, for she is too proud, though but a lowly peasant, to let the* **Lady Harriet** *see her cry. She sees the blood on* **Harriet***'s hands.*) Aaaaaah! Blood!

**Harriet** Yes . . . I . . .

**Molly** Enough! Murderer! Assassin! Savage! Do not sully these green woods with your red red words!

**Harriet** But . . madam . . . I . .

**Molly** Silence! Never speak to me again! Never open your mouth again in my presence! Never come near me again! From the first moment I set eyes on you, I have hated you from the very bottom of my heart! Lady Harriet Helstone . . I call down a curse on you! May the blood that this day you have shed of this innocent fox be repaid a hundred nay a thousand times. May the Helstone blood flow like a storm-swollen river through your halls. May it flow to the sea and wash, wash away the family of Helstone from the memory of all humanity! May your family never prosper, never be happy, never be merry. May you never marry! May you never ever ever *ever* hunt again!!!

*She exits.*

**Harriet** Damn you . . . I tried! I went against my blood, my class, my lineage, my character to save that wretched fox! I flung myself, uncaring of my favourite riding habit before M'father, M'mother, M'brother's mounts. Painted, powdered Lady Adelia Beasley smirked . . . . 'What's this . . . a damn lily-liver?' 'No, not that, never that' I cried. But they let loose the dogs . . . canine mouths slavered canine mouths opened . . . shut . . . tore that fox from my very arms and . . . and . . . and Thunder And Lightning!!!! It was but a Paltry Fox!!!! Jervis . . . bring Thunderer about . . I would ride away!!!!

*There is a sound of thundering hooves, whinnies. She exits.*

Hold him still! Kneel down Jervis! Without a mounting stool I must needs use your back!

*The hooves canter away.*

### Chapter Four: A Buxom Young Wench and A Sprightly Old Woman

*Two scenes now unfold simultaneously. The first is **Lady Harriet**'s dressing room, the second is the cheery, simple but specklessly clean cottage where **Molly** lives.*

**Lady Harriet** *enters the first scene.*

**Harriet** God's Wounds!! Hare 'n' Hounds!! Thunder 'n' Turf! What a *vile* humour possesses me . . Betsy! Come and change me! Where is that demn gel?

**Betsy** *enters. Although in these penurious times she may* seem *physically similar to **Molly Penhallow** . . . she is a* completely different *character. Born in Cheapside, she is a pert member of the serving classes.*

**Betsy** Here I am, Mum! Lawks-a-mercy, Milady, look how you've a-ruined your grand gown! I'm sure I don't know how I'm to sponge and mop all the blood and mud out of that fine raiment to be sure!

**Harriet** Silence, babbler! Curb your pert tongue and busy yourself with pulling off my boots!

**Betsy** Yes, Mum! Mercy, Milady . . how tight they are! Tight as a tinker's trailer and no mistake! I need the strength of ten costermongers for this task and no mistake!

*She pulls off the boots.*

**Harriet** Mistake . . mistake? I have had enough of mistakes today . . so hold your tongue!

**Betsy** Yes, Milady! There Milady! Off in a trice!

**Harriet** Undo me!

**Betsy** Yes, Mum! (*She undoes* **Lady Harriet**.) I'll take these dirty boots to the boot boy, milady . . . he's out there a-collecting the ladies and gentlemen's boots of all the ladies and gentlemen's ladies and gentlemen!

*She exits.*

**Harriet** I am wild with rage! See how my breast heaves! Feel how my heart pounds! My skin burns with fury!

*As her jacket is undone, we can probably see all this.*

That girl! That ridiculous, stupid, ignorant, uneducated, untitled girl! Where did she go? How dare she leave before I dismissed her? How dare she dash away to . . . where . . a hovel I suppose . . . a nasty, low, dirty cote in the village I suppose . . I suppose there is a village down there in the valley . . . I suppose she is there even now . . . surrounded by her low folk . . telling her snivelling tale . . .

*As* **Harriet** *muses in her splendid room* **Molly** *enters her specklessly clean cottage.*

**Molly** Ah, home at last! Granny! Oh, Granny dearest . . . I'm home! Where is she? Out gathering faggots I daresay, for our supper fire! I'll see if I can spy her from the window!

*Meanwhile . . . .*

**Harriet** Oh, I cannot sit still! Where is that girl??? I will go and pace my room until she returns!

*She exits.*

*Meanwhile . . . .*

**Molly** No, nowhere to be seen . . it's perhaps as well . . . there is such turmoil in my heart that I must calm its storms or dear old Granny will be tossed on my inner seas! That lady! That rude, cruel, arrogant, overweening, proud lady! How could she? How could she kill my fox friend? I expect she has mounted her horse . . and ridden off up that high hill . . to where? . . . to Helstone Hall I suppose . . . and she is sitting there now with all her mighty and powerful friends . . . laughing at my plight . . sneering at my red-haired friend's death . . . Oh Granny, there you are.

*Although in these penurious times it may seem that* **Granny** *looks not unlike* **Lady Harriet**, *she is in fact a completely different character being a cheery, nut-cheeked, wise old villager who, unlike her granddaughter, speaks in simple peasant vernacular.*

**Molly** Ah, you have found some faggots for the fire!

**Granny** Oh yes my little nutkin! I been by the hedgerows and ditchrows a-foraging and a-faggoting. And regard . . . a goodsome armful for a warm and zumly fire.

*I wouldn't be surprised if* **Granny** *didn't pronounce all her 'f's as 'v's. And, not to put too fine a point on it . . all her 's's as 'z's!*

But cushla-cushla . . . look at these tears . . . rolling down your hazel-down cheeks like streams to a river!

**Molly** They are nothing Granny. Just tears for the place of us poor peasantry in the very flattest plain of the landscape we call society . . and God's poor animal kind below that even! While up on the green hills folk who would call themselves *gentle* hurl sticks and stones of privilege and scorn!

**Granny** Cushla-cushla, lambkin-mine, I cannot see through the thickets and hedges of these fancy book-learning words for the speckled eggs of truth in your chest nest!

**Molly** I'm sorry, Granny. It's all my schooling which my rich Aunt spent all those golden sovereigns upon. I declare, I've quite lost the clear, easy, country way of speaking like you!

**Granny** Ah, upson-downson, my darling bud of May . . . why don't you ramble down to the brook and wash your eyes clear . . .

**Molly** I will.

**Granny** . . . and then tell Granny-goodie all about it!

**Molly** *exits.*

**Granny** It'll be something to do with men and field and lane mischief . . . mark my words, zum lovesome lad has crept his harvest hand into my little haywain's cornstook!

*Meanwhile . . . .*

**Betsy** (*off*) Oh Milady . . . I've told that boot boy to be sure and a-rub down your boots first after old Sir Helstone . . otherwise he'll feel the sharp end of my tongue and no mistake! (*Enters.*) . . and now to take off all that fine attire . . . Milady . . Milady? Where is she?

*Meanwhile . . . .*

**Granny** Now, I'll go out with these kindlins and faggots and break them up into firey-sticks to warm my baby lambkin!

*She exits.*

*Meanwhile . . . .*

**Betsy** Ah . . . I spot Milady . . . pacing up and down, down and up before her long windows which overlook his Lordship's deer park! Pardon me, Mum, but would Milady like me to lug ten buckets of hot water up the four flights of stairs for a bath for you?

**Harriet** (*off*) What? . . . Who? . . . Where? . . . Oh. I was in a reverie! Who calls?

**Betsy** 'Twas I, Milady . . . Your pert Cheapside maid!

**Harriet** (*off*) Oh, Betsy . . 'tis you!

**Betsy** 'Tis I! Would Milady like me to lug ten buckets of hot water up the four flights of stairs for a bath for you?

**Harriet** (*entering*) Why not?

**Betsy** Why not indeed . . *Miladyship*? I'll go down to the well then, Milady . . .

**Harriet** Wait Betsy! I am in the humour for listening to your Cheapside wisdom!

**Betsy** Very well, Milady. On what matter, Milady?

**Harriet** On the matter of . . . love. Why love? Why do questions of love throb a threnody across the strings of my heart? It must be Lord Rothermere . . or someone I've yet to meet . . . Betsy . . . have you ever been in love?

**Betsy** Love, Milady? *Me*, Milady? Why . . Milady . . . what with Lord Rothermere, Lord Harry Squiffley, Sir Ranulph Dukes, even dear senile old Lord Helstone your dear father . . catching me in every nook, cranny and window embrasure in the stately pile, saying 'just be kind to this gentrified member, mi dear' . . what with the stable staff liking to pounce on me from behind every stallion and mare . . saying 'look at this grarss-snake I found . . un's rearing up' . . . . what with after I've retired from putting you to bed at two in the morning . . . I've got the boot boys, the gentlemen's gentlemen, even Mr Dunsey the butler a-forcing their way into my unlocked door and up my unbleached nightdress . . saying 'how's about *this* for a warming-pan handle?' And then I've got to be up at six a-hot-ironing your fine dresses! No, no, no Milady . . . we servants are not gentle enough for love!

**Harriet** I suppose not! Ah Betsy . . . it is so much harder for we gentry!

**Betsy** Milady.

**Harriet** I'll have my bath now.

**Betsy** Milady.

*She exits.*

**Harriet** Ah . . . where is love? They say love tames. They say love soothes the unquiet heart. They say love is a deer which stands in the forest glade and the lion, the tiger, the wolf kneel down before its gentleness and the air about the forest glade is green and clear. Why am I thinking of love? I'll stop. There . . . I've stopped. I'll have my supper and think of food. And then . . . I'll do . . charitable works just as Mama wishes me to do . . . I'll take that poor peasant girl I met this afternoon some gift to show that I do have a heart! Yes . . that's what I shall do!

*She exits.*

*Meanwhile . . . . .*

**Molly** Oh, I am so refreshed by my dip in the brook! Yet not refreshed! Granny! Granny! Out breaking up the firey-sticks I shouldn't wonder! I'll sit here and muse till she returns and then I can pour out my heart to her about that accursed Lady Helstone! Yes . . . I shall muse . . . On what? I'll muse . . . on love. Why love? They say love excites. They say love awakens the sleeping heart. They say love is a tiger which walks in the forest glade and the lamb, the deer, the goat put their heads in its open mouth and the air in the forest glade is red and hot. Why am I thinking about love? I'll stop. There . . . I've stopped. I'll have my supper and think of food. And then . . . I'll make a corn dolly . . . just as Granny likes me to . . . and I'll make one like that grand Milady and throw her on the fire . . . Yes . . . that's what I shall do!


### The First Broken-Hearted Woman Sings an Angry Song


**Harriet** *enters reading* Her Aching Heart.

**Harriet** (*reading*) 'I'll make a corn dolly . . just as Granny likes me to . . . and I'll make one like that grand Milady and throw her on the fire . . . Yes . . . that's what I shall do!' . . .

*She laughs.*

Yeah . . . go for it! Burn that grand Milady!

*She sighs. She sings . . .*

*Song: Good Manners*

Sally came from the North
She met Jane on a train
They clicked right away
They'd got plenty to say
They conversed without any strain
They had
Good manners
Good manners
That's what you need
  nice couple
  fun twosome

Soon, hey, they were doing it
Got in, switched out the light
And with no screaming
Eyes closed as if dreaming
And they did it only at night
They had
Good manners
Good manners
That's what you need
  nice couple
  fun twosome

Well Jane gets bored with this scene
She starts dating Louise
They're both on the floor
Sally walks through the door
She'd have knocked but Jane gave her the keys
She had
Good manners
Good manners

That's what you need
   nice couple
   fun threesome

Jane says 'This is Louise
She just lives down the street'
Sally gets a knife
And ends Louise's life
With a wound in her heart, she's so neat
She had
Good manners
Good manners
That's what you need
   nice ending
   fun funeral . . . .

*She stops singing.*

 Oh . . . Fuck It!!!

*She reads the book again.*

'There . . . that's the corn dolly finished at last . . . now to throw it on the fire . . .'

*She exits reading.*


**Chapter Five: High and Low**

**Molly** *has been making a corn dolly during the last song.*

**Molly** There . . . that's the corn dolly finished at last . . . now to throw it on the fire . . . (*She looks at it.*) But it's so beautiful . . so perfect . . . so . . . this is the finest corn dolly I've ever made . . . it looks like . . . it looks like . . (*Guess who it looks like.*)

*There is a sound of the thundering hooves belonging to six horses pulling a racing Perch-Phaeton.*

What's that? A carriage passing by so late at night? What ho . . . it's stopping close by. (*It is . . .*) It must be some of the young rakes from Helstone Hall coming to watch a cock fight in the back room of 'The Jolly Wreckers' . . our local hostelry . . .

*She returns to her corn dolly.*

*Off, we hear an exchange of voices.*

**Harriet** (*off*) Sirrah, lowly old crone . . . Direct me to the humble cottage of the young maid with the flaxen hair who this day disrupted the Helstone Hunt!

**Granny** (*off*) Why gentle lady, she mun live behind the rose-grown wattle and daub of thiz very fragrant herb bed! Her name be Molly Penhallow . . . And she mun be my lovesome grandchilder!

**Harriet** (*off*) Then bend your back so I may use you as a step to descend from this coach!

**Molly** (*who has been listening to this exchange*) Why . . . I declare . . . the ankle of this corn dolly is not quite straight! (*She twists the corn dolly's ankle slightly.*)

*Off we hear . . . .*

**Harriet** (*off*) Aaaaaaaaaagh!!!

**Molly** There!

**Harriet** (*off*) Damme . . . I have turned my ankle on your rounded old back, crone!

**Granny** (*off*) Lord love you fine lady . . I am old . . . there was a time when I could take the full weight of many a fine gentleman and lady on my strong yeowoman's shoulders!

**Harriet** (*off*) Silence! Hold my horses while I limp into yonder low cottage!

**Granny** (*off*) Oh what fine beasts! Cushla-a-cushla you fine stallions!

**Harriet** Is it this way? . . . (*She limps in.*) Ah . . . there you are.

**Molly** Yes Madam.

**Harriet** I have had naught but ill-luck since you cursed me so roundly in the thorn thicket! The bath my maid Betsy prepared scalded me . . . At dinner I was seated next to deaf Lady Aurelia Dumbarton on the one side, burping, belching and farting Lord

Sir Jingo Wakefield on t'other! I had no appetite for the Soup à
la Reine removed with fillets of turbot, with an Italian sauce; the
chickens à la Tarragon flanked by a dish of spinach and
croutons, the glazed ham, cold partridges, some broiled
mushrooms and the braised mutton pie. Even the baskets of
pastries, the Rhenish cream, the jelly, the Savoy cake, the dish of
salsify fried in butter, the omelette and the anchovy sauce failed
to tempt me. The champagne was flat. The burgundy heavy.
Dunsey, the oaf, dropped Rhenish cream on my blue and I had
to change into my white! I went down to the stables and
Thunderer had cast a spavin! And now I've turned my ankle on
that wretched crone's back!

**Molly** What care I for all that? Save that the wretched crone is
my beloved grandmother.

**Harriet** Thunder 'n' Turf!!! I'll throw her some sovereigns when
I leave!

**Molly** Then throw them now. There is the door.

**Harriet** I have brought you something.

**Molly** I want nothing of you.

**Harriet** This you will. 'Tis a young roe deer from my father's
park. Its mother died in a . . . cooking accident. It must be
suckled. All creatures of the park and forest love you. (*Long
pause.*) You will tend it and stroke it and kiss its downy head.
(*Long pause.*) You will let it suck milk from your fingers and
nibble at your palm. (*Long pause.*)

**Molly** All creatures of the park and forest . .

**Harriet** . . . love you. Yes.

**Molly** I will . . .

**Harriet** . . . tend it and . .

**Molly** . . . stroke it and . . .

**Both** . . . kiss its downy head.

**Harriet** Yes.

**Molly** I will let it . .

**Harriet** . . suck . . .

**Molly** . . . milk from my fingers and . .

**Harriet** . . nibble . . .

**Molly** . . . at my . . .

**Harriet** . . . palm. Palm.

**Molly** Where is this . . . deer?

**Harriet** In my . . . . Perch-Phaeton.

*She goes to get the deer.*

**Molly** Oh what is happening? What is happening? (*In her confusion, she twists the limbs of her corn dolly.*) I am all . . . awry! I am all at sea! Within I am storm-tossed!

*Off, we hear . . .*

**Harriet** (*off*) AAgh . . what is happening to me . . My limbs are not my own . . They are twisted this way and that way as if by some supernatural force!

**Granny** (*off*) Lord love you, Milady . . have a care! I cannot hold these horses if you mun dance around so in front of un!

**Harriet** (*off*) Hold the horses fool! Oh, how sea-sick I feel! I'll take out the roe deer while you . . Oh, I am twisted again . .

**Granny** (*off*) Milady . . if you fall upon me so with yon roe deer in your arms I mun can't stay these frisky stallions!

*There is the sound of hooves ploughing, horses neighing, a Perch-Phaeton being pulled back and forth over something soft. There is a heart-rending scream, reminiscent of a young animal in anguish. Then silence.*

**Granny** (*off*) Oh . . Milady!!

**Harriet** *enters with a limp-looking roe deer in her arms.*

**Harriet** I do naught around you but cover myself in the blood of forest creatures.

**Molly** Give the deer to me.

*She takes it.*

**Molly** Ah . . . it's still warm. I'll lay it here . . before the glowing fire. Stand back Madam . . . you have done enough this night!

**Harriet** *stands back.*

**Harriet** How firm she is!

**Molly** Let me observe this soft body . .

**Harriet** How softly she looks . . .

**Molly** Let me feel this tiny . . . *beating*! . . heart . . .

**Harriet** How the firelight warms her red cheeks . . .

**Harriet** *might be taking snuff at this time.*

**Molly** If I gently rub here . . . on this creature's breast . . . .

**Harriet** Oh . . . . her hands!

**Molly** And try to breathe some life into its tender mouth . . .

**Harriet** She kisses . . . .

**Molly** Oh, she breathes . . . her breast swelled and she took in air . . and, oh look . . not dead . . . but merely in a swoon!

*The deer perks up.*

*The following speeches together . . . as* **Harriet** *crouches by the deer and she and* **Molly** *excitedly seize each other's hands.*

**Molly** Oh look . . the dear, dear thing . . . its large eyes look up so trustingly . . . its gentle soul stares into mine . . . its breast heaves with life . . . oh I am overcome!

**Harriet** Oh look . . . the dear, dear thing . . . its large eyes look up so trustingly . . . its gentle soul stares into mine . . its breast heaves with life . . . oh I am overcome!

**Harriet** *is not referring to the deer. They are holding hands.*

**Molly** I am so glad it is alive!

**Harriet** What is alive?

**Molly** The deer . . .

**Harriet** Oh the deer. Yes.

**Molly** Milady . . . you hold my hands . .

**Harriet** Oh . . so I do!

**Molly** Loose them . . if you will.

**Harriet** Of course. (*She does.*) Tralala!

**Molly** And take your deer back to your father's deer park.

**Harriet** But I brought him for . . .

**Molly** I cannot accept him. I hate you from the bottom of my heart. Please go.

**Harriet** Look into my eyes and say that . .

**Molly** Please go.

**Harriet** The part about hate . .

**Molly** (*looks into her eyes*) I . . . . . . . . (*Long pause.*)

**Harriet** Yes . . . ?

**Molly** . . . hate . . . you . . . from the . . . bottom of my heart.

**Harriet** *seizes* **Molly** *by the arms.*

**Harriet** Listen to me, peasant!!! I will not have it! Will not have this hate for me! I will turn it into something else though what I know not! And mark this . . . Madam . . I am the wilful, spoilt impetuous Lady Harriet Helstone of Helstone Hall and I always . . *always* Get Whatso'er I Want!!!

**Molly** And mark this . . . Lady Harriet Helstone . . (*As she says this she flings off* **Harriet**'s *hands and stands tall.*) I am Molly Penhallow of Penhallow Hollows . . . and I never . . . *never* . . Give In To Anyone!!! Here . . . (*She thrusts the deer into* **Harriet**'s *arms.*) Now go!

**Harriet** I will! But I shall return!

**Molly** You will not. You shall not return!

*The deer follows this exchange.*

**Harriet** Madam . . you have met your match!

**Molly** And you Madam . . . have met yours!

**Harriet** *exits.*
**Molly**, *in fury, picks up the corn dolly . . . she hurls it to the floor.*

*Off we hear . . .*

**Harriet** (*off*) Open that Perch-Phaeton door!
Bend your back woman . . .
Aaagh . . . I am hurled to the floor!
Catch the deer . . . catch i . . . . .

*There is a ploughing of hooves, frightened whinnying and a horrifying crunch . . as of a young roe deer being run over by a Perch-Phaeton wheel. Silence. Then . . . .*

**Granny** Oh. Lord love you . . . lackaday . . . see how that poor little deer a-flew through the air and landed upson-downson right under your carriage wheels Milady!!

**Harriet** Out of my way . . . peasant!!!

*The carriage drives off.*


## The Second Broken-Hearted Woman Sings a Restless Song

*As the carriage drives off,* **Molly**, *furious, struggles out of her clothes. Underneath she is wearing a T-shirt and tracksuit. She sings.*

*Song: Restless*

**Molly**
It's hot, it's late, it's dark
Hey wasn't that the door?
I thought I heard something
I though I saw . . .
Jumpy . . .
Restless . . .
A cat? A dog? A shape?
That creaking floor
I thought I heard something
I thought I saw

There's a face at the window
There's a hand on the door

It's here, it's there, it's gone
I don't believe in ghosts
I thought I heard something
I thought I saw . . .
Jumpy
Restless
It's white, it's grey, it's there
I don't believe in them
I thought I heard something
I thought I saw . . .

There's someone out there somewhere
With a hand on the door . . .

Fuck it . . . Oh fuck it! (*She picks up* Her Aching Heart *reads*.) 'The
Perch-Phaeton bearing the Lady Harriet sped through the dark
night . . . in the corner . . on the plush seat . . . Harriet leaned
back discontentedly against the squabs . . . . .'

**Harriet** *enters, wearing an old towelling dressing gown. She is reading*
Her Aching Heart.

**Harriet** ' . . . Molly sat in the now-dying embers of the cottage
fire . . . the rush candles barely lit the simple room . . .'

*As she reads . . .* **Molly** *picks up the phone and dials.*

' . . . Molly's mind was a turmoil of emotions . . . of heartbreak
for the fox, of yearning for the baby roe deer . . but most of all . .
there was burning hatred for Lady Harriet Helstone . . .'

**Harriet**'s *telephone rings. She picks it up.*

Hello?

**Molly** Hello . . . hi . . . it's Molly . . . we met at the LGCIF
confer . . .

**Harriet** Oh yes, hello, how are you?

**Molly** Oh . . you know . . .

**Harriet** Oh yes.

**Molly** So. What you up to?

**Harriet** Oh me. Well . . . I'm *reading*.

**Molly** Oh no! Me too! What you reading?

**Harriet** It's called *Her Aching Heart*.

**Molly** Oh no! Me Too!!!

**Harriet** No????

**Molly** Yes!!!! Isn't that weird??? Where you up to?

**Harriet** (*reads*) 'The Perch-Phaeton bearing the Lady Harriet sped through the dark night . . .' She's just totalled the deer . . . where are you up to?

**Molly** (*reads*) 'Molly's heart was a turmoil of emotions . . .'

**Harriet** I wonder why?

**Molly** She's feeling hatred for Lady Harriet . . .

**Harriet** Oh, sure!

**Molly** So, do you think they're in love?

**Harriet** No!!!!!!

**Molly** Poor fuckers!

**Harriet** Yes!

**Molly** So, listen, anyway . . . are you doing anything Thursday?

**Harriet** No . . no, I'm not.

**Molly** So . . do you fancy doing anything?

**Harriet** Me? Oh . . . . .

**Molly** Well . . . we could do something nice.

**Harriet** That would be nice.

**Molly** So I'll think of something, shall I . . and ring you . . Wednesday . .

**Harriet** Okay. That'd be nice.

*There is a pause.*

**Molly** Well . . . back to your book . . .

**Harriet** Back to yours.

**Molly** Goodnight.

**Harriet** Goodnight.


**Two Women With Hearts on the Mend Sing a Song**

*Song: It's Spring – Hearts Mend*

Crawling out from under a stone
An egg-white termite blinks at the light
A slug tracks across a leaf
Its shiny trail shines in the weak sun
Black dots before my eyes in the garden
I'm not dizzy, they're early gnats
The surface of the pond is bubbling and frothing
Frogs clinging together
Tadpole jelly on its way

It's spring
Hearts mend
Why not sing?

Hung like millions of mighty hammocks
Cobwebs in the corners of all my rooms
Blowing like tumbleweed in Kansas
The fluff under my bed's a disgrace
Like the Plimsoll line on a ship
The black tidemark on my bath must go
Like what leaked from the *Torrey Canyon*
The grease on my cooker could kill a seal
Spring-cleaning is on its way

It's spring
Hearts mend
Why not sing?

Eating less Kit-Kat's and Cheesy Quavers
Losing a couple of pounds
Walking to work every single morning
Going to Dancercise every week
Buying the *Guardian* not the *Mirror*

Reading only improving books
To the launderette before the pile's gigantic
Never wearing knickers twice
New beginning is on its way

It's spring
Hearts mend
Why not sing?

*The song builds to a stirring crescendo.*

# Act Two

## Chapter Six: A Fop

*A fop's room.* **Lord Rothermere** *enters with many starched neckerchiefs. He is trying to tie one round his neck. Although in these penurious times he may bear a* passing *resemblance to* **Molly** *in a curly black wig he is a* completely different person.

**Rothermere** M'name's Rothermere . . . Peer of The Realm! and I'm trying to tie m'damn neckerchief! (*He spoils one.*) Damme! (*Hurls it to the floor, takes another.*) I'm trying to achieve *The Waterfall* . . But the damn thing looks more like the Ruddy *Rain Butt.* Haw Haw Haw! M'rusticating here with The Helstones because m'pockets are to let! Mortgaged m'family seat on a curricle race and I lorst. Haw Haw Haw! So I'm down here courting The Lady Harriet . . . trying to cut a dash! (*He spoils another one. Hurls it to the floor.*) Damme! (*Takes another.*) She's a damn shrew . . . but she's good bloodstock and she's worth twenty thousand a year so m'pressing m'suit! She's no plain Jane so I don't mind mounting the filly and riding her hard to the bridle and curbing her to rein if you get m'meaning! Zounds . . . think I've done it! (*He lowers his chin carefully over the Waterfall.*) Splendid! Splendid!!!! Thing is . . . this hellcat's rather hard to bring about to the *bit* of late . . . Winces when I steal a buss . . Snarls when I put m'hand to her bodice . . No matter . . . L'offer for her . . . bed her . . get her breeding . . . the friskiest mare trots to harness once she's in foal! (*He has been putting on his coat, his quizzing glass.*) I'll take the whip to her this very eve after supper!

*He exits.*

## Chapter Seven: A Yokel

*A yokel enters with a bunch of simple hedgerow flowers. Although in these penurious times he may bear a* passing *resemblance to* **Harriet** *in a red wig he is a* completely different *character.*

**Joshua** Oi'm Joshua, good gentlefolk and ladies! Oi'm stable laad up at Helstone Hall . . and Oi'm a-taking these hedgerow blooms to Penhallow Hollows cos I'm a-courtin!!! Father said 'Are ee after old Granny Penhallow then?' and I roars and says '*No* father . . her's too *oldsome*! Oi'm arfter Miss Molly!' And ee, Farther, says, 'You go careful now young laad, they Penhallows look red as roses but they got briars as I know when Oi troied to tumble Miss Molly's Maa . . . she put up a devil of a foight till I tied er with some hedging twine . . . ere . . I ope when I caught 'er tweren't about nine months afore Molly were dropped on straw . . else an' she's yore sister!!!' And I said 'Oi don't care an she's my sister, Farther, for that would make us close and anyway what do it matter, you'm tied every woman in this village with yore hedging twine so any lass moight be moi sister!' Oi love Miss Molly sore. Her's all the world to me.

*Meanwhile, in the present day, the phone rings.* **Harriet** *goes to answer it.*

**Harriet** Hello? Hi . . hello! I'm fine. How are you? Yeah . . . I did get to work on time . . just! Yes . . . it was nice. Yes . . . . me too. I was going to ring you tonight . . . see if you fancied . . . You don't know what I was going to say! Yes . . . that was what I was going to say! Yes . . . you come to me this time . . it's only fair! (*She smiles.*) Yes . . that would be fine . . . perfect. About then then. 'Bye. 'Bye. (*She puts down the phone.*)

*Meanwhile,* **Molly Penhallow** *enters with something cupped in her hands.*

**Joshua** (*covered with confusion*) Oh, Fence and Stoyle . . . here comes Miss Molly now!

**Molly** Oh Joshua . . . I was conversing with this fledgling which lives in the old oak tree in the lane . . . and it leaned so far over the nest side to hear my murmurings that it did fall out onto the lane and I fear it is in a swoon!

**Joshua** Oh Miss Molly . . . how all woild creatures do love ee . . . put it down on the ground here . . I will help ee make all better.

**Molly** Oh Joshua . . . how kind you are . . how full of gentleness!

*She lays the fledgling down on the ground before* **Joshua**. *He lifts up his foot and stamps on it.*

**Joshua** There . . . Miss Molly . . . that's put the little thing out of its misery! Here . . . Oi brought you these hedgerow blossoms . . . they are for . . . besoide yore bed.

**Molly** *takes the hedgerow blossoms.*

**Molly** Joshua . . . Take that. (*She brings down the bunch on his head.*) And that . . . (*She knees him in the groin.*) And that . . . (*She punches him on the chin.*)

**Joshua** Miss Molly . . .

**Molly** Is all the world mad??? Cannot all things *live*??? Cannot all things *be*??? A bird . . a deer . . . a fox . . . all dead? Ah . . . everything swims in blood!!!!

*She runs off.*

**Joshua** A bird . . .
(*He sees the bird, what's left of it.*)
A deer? . . . . a deer????
A fox? . . . . . a fox????
I don't remember stamping on no deers and foxes!
She mun be in a fever of some sort.
Oh lord . . . her's put oi in a daze . .
Which way am I walking . . .

*He exits.*

*As* **Joshua** *wanders dazedly off, the present-day* **Molly** *returns engrossed in* Her Aching Heart.

**Molly** (*reads*) ' . . . the gentle giant was in a daze. Why had she served him thus? Why had she dealt him those unjust blows? He was a simple man . . . honest, true, with no deceit . . . he saw, but could not comprehend, her anguish. He knew it could not be for the bird, though for the bird . . and the creatures of the wild wood it seemed to be . . . he shrugged and followed her down the lane . .

*During this read account . . .* **Joshua** *might make some confused sounds offstage to show his confusion.*

as the sad youth strolled despondently away . . . in the arbour of
the darkly-forbidding, ivy-covered Helstone Hall . . . standing
under the leafy canopy of oak, beech, elm, silver birch,
laburnum, sycamore, ash, willow, hawthorn, Douglas fir,
Norway spruce, Austrian pine . . oh come on . . . enough with
the trees! . . . the discontented Lady Harriet sighed at the
waxing moon . . .'

*She exits.*

## Chapter Eight: A Misfortune

**Lady Harriet** *enters.*

**Harriet** Ah . . me . . . . (*Sighs.*) Lackaday! (*Sighs.*) Oh moon . . .
when you look down on me with your pale silvery face cover'd
o'er with dark-scudding clouds . . what do you see? You see
yourself in me! I am become you . . . a pale planet that
circumnavigates this globe, the earth look you, not there, not
there at all when the sun shines . . . and then, at night I rise . . .
clamber slowly behind the clouds up, up into the star-tossed sky
. . . to hang like a pearl upon a maiden's breast . . . rising and
falling with her ululating breath . . . . oh . . . I am become quite
moonsick! What do I seek? To conquer . . . yes. To invade . . .
oh yes. To colonise . . . oh yes yes yes! But to conquer . . invade
. . . colonise . . . what? What do I seek? Where do I seek? Who
do I seek?

*During the last eight lines,* **Lord Rothermere** *has appeared and listens
to her mooning.*

**Rothermere** Stap me . . . the filly's in heat! Now to get m'feet in
her stirrups . . m'thighs gripped tight around her steaming
shanks and ride ride ride! (*He steals up behind her, puts his hands on
her breasts.*) What ho, Lady Harriet!

**Harriet** AAAgh! (*Looks down at the hands.*) Oh . . . what ho, Lord
Rothermere. Take your bejewelled hands off m'fichu.

**Rothermere** Or what, Madam?

**Harriet** Or I will bend back the finger on which rests the Rothermere Ruby and it will snap like a chicken leg.

*He takes away his hands.*

I am not in the humour for social intercourse, My Lord.

**Rothermere** 'Twas not *social* intercourse I had in mind, My Lady.

**Harriet** What then?

**Rothermere** I have this hour had private word with your father in the library, sweet lady. Because of my fine lineage, my owning of two counties . . and the relative lack of madness in m'family . . he has encouraged me to press m'suit and offer you m'hand, m'heart . . . and any other of m'manly parts in marriage!

**Harriet** Marriage?

**Rothermere** Ay . . marriage . . . and all that goes with the mingling together of bloodlines!

**Harriet** I do not wish to marry, Sir.

**Rothermere** Come come, m'dear . . you are not in your first bloom of youth . . . good men are hard to find.

**Harriet** 'Tis true.

**Rothermere** Your father says I am to insist . . Lady . . I have the starting price . . now race with me!

**Harriet** I will not, Sir!

**Rothermere** Madam, you will!

*He lunges for her, she throws him off.*

**Harriet** No!

**Rothermere** Yes!

*He lunges again. She throws him off.*

**Rothermere** Yes!

**Harriet** No!
Sir . . if you snatch at me again . .
I shall have no recourse but to defend myself . . .

**Rothermere** With what my lady?
The arbour is secluded . . . and the house guests all playing
billiards!

**Harriet** With . . . with . . . oh . . . with this sword so fortuitously
discarded earlier today by my brother Harry!

*She picks up the fortuitously discarded sword.*

**Rothermere** Cross swords with me, would you, Milady?
Very well! (*He draws his sword, which luckily he had decided to wear to
supper that evening.*) I will fence thee into a corner, into a sweat,
into a swoon and then into a bed! *En garde!*

**Harriet** *En garde!*

*They fence. Obviously if they can cut candles in two, swing from
chandeliers, do stunts etc . . . This would be favourite.*

**Rothermere** *nicks* **Harriet** *on the arm.*

**Rothermere** Ah . . first blood!
I will draw other blood from ye yet, lady!

**Harriet** (*recovering bravely*) That ye will not, fight on!

*They fight on.* **Harriet** *lands a fatal body thrust.*

**Rothermere** What? Who? How?
You have slain me!
So ends the line of Rothermere . . .
So empties that fine stable . .
Off canters the last . . . stallion . .

*He dies.*

**Harriet** No . . . do not die! Curse you . . you sack of malmsy . .
live!! Live!!!! He's dead! Damme damme damme!!! What can I
do? I'll hide him . . here . . under this . . . (*She checks.*) Betula
pendula . . . (*She drags him off.*) Oh, how my wound pains me!
But it is as naught compared with the agony in my heart . . .
what am I to do? The house is full of Rothermere's cronies . . See
them, by the light of many candles, a-playing billiards . . . if they
knew what I have just done . . . they would lay me on that green
field of baize . . and with their great cues shoot their balls into

my body's pockets . . . such is our class's notion of after-supper sport! Who to turn to? . . . My father . . . I have killed a suitor! . . . My mother . . . was dallying with Rothermere . . . Oh, what an ill-starred woman I am! Breathless, Friendless and Helpless. It is all the fault of that pretty peasant! All from her curse! She shall learn humility . . . desperation and agonising pain. I shall go to her cottage and . . . and kill her too!!!!

*She exits.*


## Chapter Ten: A Lowly Bed

**Molly** *enters, she is wearing a cloak.*

**Molly** What a strange, wild night it is! I have been out wandering amid the sights and sounds and smells of the darkness . . . such sights I have seen . . . such sounds I have heard . . such smells I have . . . I found myself in my restless roaming close by Helstone Hall . . . what took me there I know not . . . and as I stared up at the first floor windows . . where . . . where the ladies of the house do sleep . . . I heard a piteous moaning in the undergrowth . . . and there lay a man . . . sore run through with a sword . . . he was at death's door . .

*There is a knocking.*

Who's that at the door?

*There is a creaking as of a door opening.*

Granny? Back from her midnight rites up at the standing stones? Aaagh?

**Lady Harriet** *enters, cloaked, with sword in hand.*

**Harriet** So! So my fine curser! So my ill fortune-teller! So my unlucky star! So . . . . Oh!!!

*She swoons in a dead faint in* **Molly**'s *arms.*

**Molly** Oh . . . you have fainted! (*She carries her to the bed.*) Oh . . . you are so hot! (*She takes off her cloak.*) Oh . . . you are hurt! (*Touches the wound.*) But not badly!

*She bathes her forehead, binds her arm, puts a cover over her, looks down at her.*


## A Woman with a Mended Heart Realises Something

**Molly** Fuck it.
Oh fuck it!

*She sings . . . .*

*Song: In Love Again*

I am not myself again
Anxious, scared, on edge again
Wondering who she's with again
Wondering where she is again
All the time in a spin again
Hours together so short again
Heart leaps when she's at the door again
Curled together on the floor again
The bed not my own again
Waiting for the phone again
Heart like a hand-grenade
Heart like a bunch of flowers
Like a just-hatched bird again
Like a recent wound again
Like a soft-boiled egg again
Like a purple bruise again
Taking taxis across town again
Damn damn damn damn
In love again.

**Molly** (*sighs then lays down beside* **Harriet**, *turns away from her on her side*) Fuck it!

**Harriet** (*wakes with a start, sees where she is, sees* **Molly**) Fuck it. Oh fuck it!

*She sings . . . .*
I am in the soup again
Sky is blue, then dark again

Fairground's come to town again
Circus with its acts again
All the time in a stew again
Grand Opera seems quite small
Fear strikes, it's the *News at Ten*
Was she there, where is she then?
My peace of mind is gone again
Words tell lies in poems again
Heart like a forest fire
Heart like a sparkling sea
Like a trampoline again
Like a traffic jam again
Like a field of flowers again
Like an upturned car again
Playing Radio Two all day again
Damn damn damn
In love again

**Harriet** (*lies down away from* **Molly**) Fuck it.

*They sleep, or so it seems. They are turned away from one another. With a sleepy sigh they both turn on their backs. They lie there. With a sleepy sigh,* **Harriet** *turns to* **Molly**. *They lie there. With a sleepy sigh,* **Molly** *turns to* **Harriet**. *They lie there. They both have a disturbing dream, or so it seems. The disturbing dream makes them toss and murmur and throw themselves into each other's arms.*

**Harriet** What? . . . .

**Molly** No . . . .

**Harriet** How? . . .

**Molly** Plea . . . . . .

**Harriet** Here . . .

**Molly** Now . . . .

**Harriet** Yes . . . .

**Molly** Yes . . . .

*They lie there.*

*They pull each other closer and closer. They begin to roll from one side to another. They swap places. They lie there. They let each other go. They turn onto their backs. They lie there . . . Then . . . They murmur and roll back. They toss and turn and roll back into their original positions. They turn away from each other. They lie there.* **Harriet** *opens her eyes.*

**Harriet** Where am I?

**Molly** You are in a lowly bed in Penhallow Hollows, Milady.

**Harriet** What am I doing there?

**Molly** You were sore wounded, Madam. . . . and you came . . . to kill me, I think.

**Harriet** Ah yes, now I remember. (*Pause.*) I have had the strangest dream.

**Molly** Oh . . . Milady?

**Harriet** I dreamed that I was in this bed awake . . . and I was lost . . . and I reached out . . . and I took a precious body . . . like mine own . . . into my arms . . and pulled her close . . . and . . held this precious body to my heart . . as though she were mine own. And then I woke and it was all a dream.

*Pause.*

**Molly** I too had the strangest dream.

**Harriet** Oh . . . Madam?

**Molly** I dreamed that I was in this bed awake . . and I was scared . . . and I reached out . . and I took a precious soul . . like mine own . . . into my arms . . . and pulled it close . . and drew this precious soul into my heart . . . as though she were mine own. (*Pause.*) And then I woke up and it was all a dream.

*Pause.*

**Harriet** It seems we have the same dream.

**Molly** It seems we do.

*They turn to face one another.*

**Harriet** Mine was no dream.

**Molly** Nor mine.

**Harriet** I was awake.

**Molly** I too.

**Harriet** What can it mean?

**Molly** I think it means we must kiss.

**Harriet** I think it must mean that too.

*They kiss.*

**Molly** I have not read of this thing in any of my wide reading!

**Harriet** Nor I.

*They kiss again.*

**Harriet** Your kiss lights up the sky with fiery rays. It fills my ears with birdsong.

**Molly** No . . . it's the dawn . . . the day races on apace . . . what brought you to my bed last night? My heart fears for you . . . Your poor arm . . . how?

**Harriet** Last eve . . I did kill a man!

**Molly** Oh! (*She clutches her breast.*)

**Harriet** He would have wedded, bedded and blood-shedded me . . .

**Molly** Oh!

**Harriet** So I slew him in fair fight! I hid his lifeless body under a Betula Pendula close by my father's house.

**Molly** Oh!

**Harriet** But mark this . . . my angel (*She swiftly kisses* **Molly**.) . . . no eyes saw our postes and ripostes . . no ears heard our panting, thus can I tell this tale which I have devised . . . I will return to the house saying that while Rothermere and I walked in the arbour . . . a savage band of smugglers fell upon us . . Rothermere defended me with his life . . . but there were too many of them and he was sadly overcome . . and run through by the leader . . a man full seven feet high . . . these blackguards then did bind me and take me as hostage . . . I was hurled to the belly of their boat . . but they, being of the lower orders . . knew not how to tie a rope . . and I unloosed myself, slid over the side . . and swam to shore . . . which I reached as the dawn rose!

**Molly** Oh!

*This 'oh' has a different ring to it.*

**Harriet** What think you of my tale?

**Molly** You say you killed this . . . Rothermere?

**Harriet** Aye.

**Molly** And you hid him under a . . .

**Harriet** Betula Pendula, aye.

**Molly** Betula Pendula . . . is that a gentrified . . Latinate name for . . . spreading birch?

**Harriet** Aye . . . what of it?

**Molly** I have a tale too, tho' not devised. Last eve . . . I wandered through the night air . . . and found myself beneath your windows . .

**Harriet** My dove!

**Molly** I stood in the trees, fearing apprehension . . and there did stumble on the still form of a man . . under a spreading birch . . he seemed at first dead . . . but I did kneel down and feeling a faint breath from his rank mouth . . . and a faint stirring from his manly chest . . . I did breathe life into him . . . just as I did the roe deer.

**Harriet** He lives?

**Molly** He lives! I hurled a stone at the window close by and gentlefolk came out and succoured him.

**Harriet** You revived him?

**Molly** Aye.

**Harriet** (*in a furious rage*) You stupid bloody PEASANT!!! Why couldn't you keep your villagey snout out of the business of your high-born betters?

**Molly** (*starting to get into a furious rage*) I beg your pardon, Madam! I had no notion when I performed my Christian deed on the poor man that you were in the habit of slaying every swain who lays a hand on you! We *villagey* maidens are more gentle!

**Harriet** You villagey maidens are more meddlesome! I now, through your interfering, face the wrath of my parents, the contempt of society . . . and a possible stretch in Newgate!!!!

**Molly** I thought only to save the poor man whom you no doubt *led* on in wilful high-bred fashion!

**Harriet** I did not kneel down and *kiss* him with my open mouth, Madam!!!!

**Molly** How *Dare* You????

**Harriet** I *Dare* Anything, Madam!!! I must now, from your necrophiliac necking . . . hatch some New Plot to Escape from these surroundings!!

**Molly** Hatch Away!!! Sit on your Big Bottom and Lay Your Foul Eggs, You Hen!!!

**Harriet** *Hen?????*
*Big Bottom????*
Yeeeaghhhh!!!

**Molly** Grrrrrraghhhhh!

**Harriet** I will to the local hostelry . . There I will turn my eyes to some oafish swain . . . I will lure him out to the barn and there, while we are dallying . . I will hit his head with a wattle and daub brick, seized from this very cote . .

**Molly** Those are my Granny's wattle and daub bricks, thief!

**Harriet** What Care I?
I will also, as *thief*, steal the oafish swain's clothes, brogues and purse. I will then to the harbour . . whence I will stow away on a

boat to France. I will rid me of this devilish country and of this devilish maiden!

**Molly** Go then!

**Harriet** I go!

**Molly** Farewell forever!!!

**Harriet** Forever, farewell!!!

*They stand staring at each other for a long time.*
**Harriet** *exits.*


## A Woman In Love Tells the World's Funniest Joke

*Song: The World's Funniest Joke*

**Molly**
On the seventh day God said
'Well, that's everything
Except I haven't had a laugh all week'
And he started chuckling . . .
'I'll create sex,' he said
'And I'll create love.'

And I'll stick them both together
And watch from up above . . .'

It's a suit that won't fit
It's a hat that's too small
It's a pair of big baggy pants
It's the world's funniest joke

It's a comic monologue
It's a sitcom dialogue
It's a punchline in the gut
It's the world's funniest joke

Hold your sides
For see
The laugh's on me

It's the skin of a banana
It's a red plastic nose
It's a custard pie in the face
It's the world's funniest joke

It's French without Saunders
It's Cannon without Ball
It's Morecambe and it's not wise
It's the world's funniest joke

God said 'I'm glad I thought of this
Amusement that I've found
To have between performing miracles,
Besides
It makes the world go round
Love messes up the sex', he said
'Sex messes up the love
And I'm a spiritual deity
Who guffaws from above'

Hold your sides
You see
The laugh's on me.

**Molly** I am sore disappointed with this secular world . . . The men are naught. The women . . . are naught. I will don this habit that dear Sister Winifred, the Scripture teacher at my school, left me in her will . . and . . (*She takes the habit, starts to put it on.*) I will enter the safe walls of the monastery of Our Lady of The Hollows on the outskirts of our village. In the warm hearts of the nuns there . . In the singing of hymns the chanting of prayers the telling of rosaries I will find my peace. (*She is dressed.*)

*The telephone rings.*

**Molly** Hello?

**Harriet** *appears, dressed in* **Joshua**'s *clothes, a little away from her.*

**Harriet** Hello, operateur . . je veux parler avec zero zero un, un, zero, un, sept huit trois, quatre quatre cinque . . .

**Molly** Hello?

**Harriet** Is that you?

**Molly** Hello . . I can hardly hear you . .

**Harriet** Hello . . . is that better?

**Molly** Better. Where are you?

**Harriet** In Lyons. I got here!

**Molly** Yes. Have you used my camping stove yet?

**Harriet** Yes! We made spaghetti on it last night!

**Molly** Did We? How are 'WE'?

**Harriet** All right. We're learning to be friends again.

**Molly** Oh. Nice.
(*She makes a face.*)
So . . . it's a nice holiday then?

**Harriet** It's all right. I miss you.

**Molly** What? The line's crackling . .

**Harriet** I miss you!!!

**Molly** I miss you too!

**Harriet** I love you!

**Molly** What? You're very faint!

**Harriet** I love you!

**Molly** I can't hear you, can you hear me?

**Harriet** Yes, I can hear you, can you hear me?

**Molly** Hello? Hello? . . . Hello? (*She listens.*) Ah . . . Monsieur . . Est-ce qu'il y a l'opérateur . . . Oh, forget it! N'importe monsieur . . au revoir! (*She puts the phone down.*)

**Harriet** Hello? Hello? Hello? Fuck it! (*She puts the phone down.*)

**Molly** *exits for the convent.*

## Chapter Eleven: Foreign Soil

**Harriet** Well, here I am in France! My plot worked like a . . .
well not like a dream . . more a nightmare . . . the clod I lured
into the barn . . whose clothes I now wear . . . had such a thick
pate I swear I had to hit him not once, not twice, but thrice to
lay him out! And he appeared not to be breathing after that!
Lackaday, what care I? What care I for ought? I am here in this
strange foreign country with a hole where once for a brief
interlude, beat my heart. I will look to the bright side. I will find
myself a job, spying for the French . . for Old Bonaparte will
surely pay me well . . . intimate as I am with all the society,
army and navy bigwigs! Now to hie me to a French Spying
headquarters . . . and take the King's shilling . . . le franc du roi
. . . le franc du Napoleon . . . oh Heavens!!

*She exits.*


## Chapter Twelve: Our Lady of the Hollows

**Molly** *comes in and kneels to prayer.*

**Molly** Ah well, Lord, here I am, on my knees again! I have now
been in these your safe walls some forty days . . . and forty long,
long, achingly long nights. The first ten days were filled with my
urgent prayers for my dear old friend Joshua . . . whose lifeless
form I came across in a barn as I made my wearisome way hither
. . . someone had savagely beaten him about the head with a
strangely familiar wattle and daub brick . . . and worse still . . .
made sport of him by dressing him in maid's attire!!! I pray
forgiveness and mercy and a taste of their own medicine for the
perpetrator of this dire deed! Luckily I chanced to feel a breath of
air from his kind mouth . . . so I did put my lips to his and
breathed life into him. He lives . . . . but I fear will never know
the joy of book-reading . . For the rest . . . Lord . . . I endeavour
with your help to banish thoughts of . . . of the secular world. I
am wearing the hair-shirt under my habit and it does take my
mind off it a morsel.

Yours faithfully,
Sister Penhallow of The Hollows


## Chapter Thirteen: An Untimely Revolution

**Harriet** *enters, dressed as a Tricoteuse . . . with revolutionary bonnet and large piece of knitting. On her feet she wears sabots.*

**Harriet** What a lucky stroke! As I was about to enter the French spying headquarters I chanced to overhear two Frenchies talking about some revolution that had occurred and it seems that we aristocrats are cursed unpopular . . . so I adopted a rough accent . . exchanged my men's attire for low foreign female tatters and here I am in the square awaiting some public event I know not what! My mind keeps wandering to England . . . to Cornwall . . to Helstone village . . to that small lowly cote . . . (*She starts knitting to take her mind off England.*) The women of the town told me to take up this dire occupation . . It keeps the hands busy but not the mind . . . and not the heart . . . what's that commotion over there? . . . A cart full of finely-featured aristocratic gentlefolk rather like m'self . . . they are taking them to that edifice . . . with the sharp blade hovering at its top . . (*She knits and watches.*) They are bending them down under it . . with their necks resting on . . Oh my God!!! (*Tumbrils, cheering and the swish of a guillotine. More cheers.*) Oh horror . . . get me out of here . . make way, lowly Frenchies . . . way for a lady!!!

*She exits.*


## Chapter Fourteen: A Nun in Torment

**Molly** *pacing up and down. She falls to her knees.*

**Molly** Is this fair, God? Two . . three kisses . . . and some almost . . *sisterly* embracing . . and for this I am in mortal agony!!! My body is on fire! Moisture courses from my eyes my armpits my . . . everywhere! It is as if someone has hatched a nest of fledglings in my lap and they are treading my nest and crying out for worms!!! What is this torture???

## Chapter Fifteen: An Aristocrat in Trouble

*Meanwhile in France . . . .* **Harriet** *chained up in a prison.*

**Harriet** The chains chafe . . . The floor is dank . . The cell is dark . . Jailers paw me. Rats gnaw me . . I am to be guillotined tomorrow. But all this is as *naught* compared to the strange unsettling disease I seem to have contracted! It is as if someone has hurled a bowl of hot soup into my loins . . . and a mouse is swimming around inside it as if 'twere a bathing pool! It is such painful, exquisite torment . . . It is such torture! I am in love with her! I cannot rest for thinking of her! I shouted and ran from her and now . . . I am served with this most miserable anguish! Wait . . who's that at the door? It's a fop . . dressed all in scarlet . . . and he carries a small flower . . . why, it's a pimpernellus rubicus . . . in common gardening lore . . . A scarlet pimpernel!

*She goes to explore.*
*She exits.*

## Chapter Sixteen: Worse Torment

**Molly** I am in love with her! I cannot rest for thinking of her! I called her 'Hen' and made mention of her Big Bottom . . and it's not so big!!!! . . . and I drove her from me to her certain death! Oh Lord . . . save her from danger! Bring her back to me . . . And I will be your servant forever!

## Chapter Seventeen: Two Nuns

*As* **Molly** *is praying . . .* **Harriet** *enters dressed as a nun.*

**Harriet** Oh how fortunate I am! The fop was no fop, but a brave and dauntless rescuer of Aristocrats caught short in The Frenchie Muddle! He brought me these religious weeds and I habited them and stole from the prison . . The Mighty Bastille! . . . and with a posse of novice nuns as cover . . . I took ship to this our

mother convent! We arrived at dead of night . . so I know not
where I am! I will discover what I can from this praying sister.

*She kneels by* **Molly**.

**Harriet** Salvete, Sister!

**Molly** Forgive me Sister . . . I know no Latin. (*She sighs.*) Save
only . . . Betula Pendula. (*She sighs again.*)

**Harriet** Which simple folk call 'Spreading Birch'.

*They look at each other.*

**Harriet** Molly.

**Molly** Harriet.

**Harriet** How?

**Molly** Where?

**Harriet** When?

**Molly** Why?

**Harriet** What care I?

**Molly** And what care I?

**Harriet** I love you.

**Molly** I love you.

*They kiss.*

**Harriet** Let us get out of this monastery . . . I have such a
strange torment in me . . .

**Molly** I also . . . But I cannot.

**Harriet** Cannot?

**Molly** I made a promise to God . . . that if He returned you safe
to me I would devote myself to Him forever.

**Harriet** You bloody stupid peasant!!!!

**Molly** '. . and she went back to London . . and Molly stayed in the monastery all her livelong days . . . and they never saw each other again. The End.'

**Harriet** That's how it finished?

**Molly** Didn't you read it?

**Harriet** I left it behind in Lyons. It was driving me crazy . . . one of them in France . . one of them in a fucking monastery!

**Molly** She was so miserable in that monastery.

**Harriet** She was fairly fucked off in France!

**Molly** Yes?

**Harriet** Yes.

**Molly** Hmm. You know when you phoned me from Lyons?

**Harriet** Yes?

**Molly** What did you want to tell me?

**Harriet** I love you.

**Molly** I love you too. Ooooh . . .

**Harriet** What . . .

**Molly** My heart hurts . . .

**Harriet** Snap.

**Both** (*reprise of* In Love Again)
I am not myself again
Ready, steady, go again
Fairground's come to town again
Circus with its acts again
All time in a spin again
Hours together so short
Heart leaps, she's at the door again
Curled together on the floor again
The bed is not my own again
I'll never sleep alone again.
Heart like a just-hatched bird

Heart like a forest fire
Like a bunch of flowers again
Like a sparkling sea again
Like a field of flowers again
Like a recent wound again
Oh, oh, my aching heart again
Hey, hey, hey hey
In love again
Ho ho, ho ho
In love again
Ha ha, ha ha
In love again
Oh oh, oh oh
In love again.

# Two Marias

**Two Marias** was first performed by Theatre Centre Women's
Company in October 1989 with the following cast:

| | |
|---|---|
| **Marguerita** | Janet Jeffries |
| **Maria** | Tracey Anderson |
| **Julia** | Rosy Fordham |
| **Maria del Morte** | Angella Wellington |

*Directed by* Libby Mason
*Designed by* Vonnie Roudette
*Music by* Jacky Tayler

*A courtyard outside a Spanish house. There are benches, chairs, terracotta pots on three sides. On the fourth side, the house. The ground is dusty. There is fierce light and heat in some of the courtyard, deep cool shade elsewhere.*

**Marguerita**, *a fifty-year-old woman, enters, carrying a bag. She looks towards the house.*

**Marguerita** This house here is full of pain.
Feel it in my heart.
Oh . . . the ache.
It answers mine.
Lay your hand upon the forehead of this house.
Flap your wings and cool the heat here.

*She sits in the deep shade on one of the benches, takes a newspaper from her bag and fans herself with it.*

**Maria**, *a young woman, enters at a rush from the house. She flings herself down on one of the benches.*

**Maria** (*absolute conviction*) I *hate* my mother!!!

**Marguerita** (*to herself*) Aye . . . dear!

**Maria** Hate her, hate her . . hate her bones and her face and her foul foul mouth!!!

*From the house we hear* **Maria**'s *mother's voice.*

**Julia** Get back in this house!

*No response from* **Maria**.

I want to talk to you!

*No response.*

Now, if not sooner!

*No response.*

Maria!!!
Please!!! (*It is not a request.*)

**Marguerita** (*to herself*) Maria!

**Maria** (*scornful*) Please!!!

**Julia** Maria!!!

**Marguerita** (*looking at the girl*) Maria . . .

**Julia** *enters from the house.*

**Julia** How *dare* you walk out when I am talking to you?

**Maria** How *dare* you talk to me like that???

**Julia** You ill-mannered little . . . bitch!!!

**Maria** You rude old . . cow!!!

**Julia** You what????

*She comes towards* **Maria**.

**Maria** Just try it, Mama!!! Just you try it!!!!

*They go to opposite sides of the courtyard, radiating hatred.*

**Julia** You cannot do this!! You cannot!!
You are my daughter and you will bring shame on me!

**Maria** I have done it! It has happened!
You're my mother! You should be pleased for me that I've . . .

**Julia** Pleased!!! Pleased for you? I should kill myself and you!!!

**Maria** I've done nothing wrong!

**Julia** Nothing wrong? God help us!

**Maria** I have fallen in *love* . . . that's all!

**Julia** Love? Love? Shut up!

**Maria** No!!!
In love . . . *love* . . . with a beautiful, wonderful, kind, intelligent
person . . . .

**Julia** Person? She is a *girl*! You can't!

**Maria** Yes, she is a girl! I can!

**Julia** You're mad!

**Maria** I'm not!

**Julia** You're sick!

**Maria** It's not a disease . . .

**Julia** You need locking up!

**Maria** It's not a crime!

**Julia** I wish you'd never been born!!!

*Absolute silence.*

**Maria** Mama.

**Julia** *looks away. Neither can speak.*

**Julia** *sees* **Marguerita** *sitting in the shade.*

**Marguerita** Just a little rest . . . then I'm on my way. Hot as hell, heh?

**Marguerita** *folds her newspaper in a certain way, takes a glass or two from her bag. Pours two glasses of water from the paper. She takes one glass to* **Julia.**

**Marguerita** Daughters, eh?

*Takes the other glass to* **Maria.**

Mothers eh? Salud!

**Julia** Señora  . . I don't think  . . this is . . .

**Marguerita** Señora . . . I'm a stranger passing through . . . It's not important.

**Maria** Not important! My life!!

**Julia** Your life? What kind of life is that??? No husband, no children, no family . . . everyone despising you? You'll have no life!

**Marguerita** Not important, I should know . . . Señorita . . . important for you of course . . . front page stuff . . . headlines ten centimetres high!

(*She reads from the newspaper.*)
'Foreign News . . . The English *Times* reports the death in
Chelmsford of a middle-class woman who had been kept
secluded in a barred and darkened house for fifty years by her
mother, who disapproved of her friendship with an army officer.'
Six lines . . . words . . this high . . for fifty years of no sun, no
freedom, no love . . . ttt . . tttt . . salud!

**Maria** It's done . . . you can't stop me.

**Julia** I'll take you to the priest . . . I'll take you to the doctor . . .
what's your father going to . . .

**Maria** You're driving me senseless!

**Julia** And what do you think you're doing to me? You're making
me crazy!!!

**Maria** You're suffocating me!

**Julia** Maria . . . Please!!!

**Maria** No!!!
I love her!

**Julia** Shut up! Shhh!

**Marguerita** (*taking out a pair of scissors and folding up a piece of
newspaper, she starts snipping*) Another small story. 'Tom Hansen,
fifteen, has taken out the first ever parental malpractice suit
against his mother and father. He is suing his parents for
$350,000, claiming they made his childhood a misery. Hansen
says he was treated so badly he will need psychiatric care for the
rest of his life.'

*She unfolds the paper. There is a line of figures.*

Tttt . . . tttt!

*She tears off the end figure carefully.*

Tom Hansen.

*She gives the figure to* **Maria**.

**Julia** I'd better make supper.

**Maria** I'm not hungry.

**Marguerita** I am.

**Julia** Señora . . excuse me . . . I . . it's not . .

**Marguerita** Convenient? It is for me . . . I'm hungry . . for food . . . for company . . . for a little sit . . .

**Maria** She can have my supper. Make it for her.

**Julia** Maria . . .

**Maria** I don't want it! And you don't want me! Not me like I am, like I really am . . . sitting down in your respectable house, eating your respectable food, at your respectable table . . .

**Julia** Shut up!

**Marguerita** This one doesn't want your food . . . you don't want this one talking  . . I want foood  . . talk . .

**Maria** Give her what she wants, Mama. Food and company for the mad woman.

**Julia** You be quiet!

**Marguerita** The mad woman.

**Julia** Señora . . . I'm sorry . . it's not . . at the moment . . it's not . . the right time.

**Marguerita** Oh it is . . . it is the right time. Please. I have brought something with me . . .

**Julia** What . . .

**Marguerita** I have brought my dead daughter.

*There is complete silence.*

**Marguerita** *takes newspaper cuttings and photographs from her bag.* She exists only here. (*She shows them.*) She lives now only in my heart. (*She sits at her bench and waits.*)

*From the bench and through the disarray of newspapers emerges her daughter,* **Maria del Morte**.

**Marguerita** Her name was Maria also. She died two years ago.

**Julia** Señora . . . I . . . what happened?

**Marguerita** This happened. Imagine it. It is a hot summer night. My daughter Maria decided to go for a swim. She said goodbye. Imagine too, that your daughter Maria also decided to go for a swim. She says goodbye. It is eight-thirty, 2 June 1987 and your Maria's car rounds the final curve that leads through the pine woods to the long beach at Punta Umbria. Suddenly, a car in the opposite lane swerves off the asphalt and throws up a shower of gravel which shatters the windscreen of the Renault behind. Blinded, the driver of the Renault veers into the oncoming lane and, at 40 miles an hour, slams into the car carrying your daughter. She breaks her ankle frantically trying to brake . . . then crushes her chest on the steering wheel as the force of the crash heaves her, face first, through the windscreen.

**Julia** God in heaven!

**Maria del Morte** I was the driver of the Renault. (*She sits down beside* **Maria**.) I too was a young woman. I too was called Maria. )

**Maria** Mama . . . I'm scared.

**Marguerita** Of course you are! You're alive!

HH**Maria del Morte** Mother . . .

**Marguerita** Yes . . . yes yes yes.

**Maria del Morte** Suppose the two of us, the drivers, were sitting side by side on a bench. I was tall and slender with light brown hair. She, like you, had a pug nose, slightly plumper . . . with short chestnut hair . . . and a brace on her teeth. Nobody could have mistaken us for each other. But that was what happened.

**Marguerita** That Saturday, two years ago, the road was jammed . . with pilgrims going to the shrine at El Roscio . . . it took the ambulance an hour to reach . . to get to the . . . the accident . . .

**Maria del Morte** By the time it arrived . . . the other girl was barely alive . . . and I was dead. We were put in the ambulance side by side and driven to the Residencia Hospital at Huelva. On the floor of the ambulance, between us, were our handbags. In the handbags were our names. Mine . . . Maria del Morte. Hers . . . Maria del Amor. In the confusion and pain and blood . . .

the handbags were switched. So, simply . . . I was pronounced alive. The other Maria was pronounced dead.

**Marguerita** At the hospital . . . the parents of Maria del Amor asked to see the body of their daughter . . . the authorities advised them against it . . . saying that the corpse was in too terrible a state . . . and they did not want them to remember their daughter that way.

**Maria del Morte** I was a dreadful sight!
(*She smiles.*)
So, while the new Maria del Morte lay ill in hospital I was buried, as Maria del Amor, in a strange cemetery, seventy miles from my home . . . mourned by a family I had never met.

*She gets up and lights candles. The smell of incense fills the courtyard.*

**Julia** What did her mother do?

**Marguerita** What would you have done?

**Julia** I would leave her room just as it was . . . the night she left for the beach . . the clothes . . all her stupid 'fashionable' clothes . . all over the bed, the chairs . . . left it untidy . . .

**Maria** It's not untidy.

**Julia** It is. You are.

**Marguerita** That is what she did.

**Julia** And at night . . I would light a candle and put it in the window, to guide her soul back through the darkness.

**Maria** I have no soul. I don't believe . . .

**Julia** You have. You do.

**Marguerita** That is what she did.

**Maria del Morte** And what of the mother of Maria del Morte?

**Marguerita** I . . . my husband . . . Antonio, my son . . . go to the hospital. She has been transferred to Seville . . . she is very ill . . . very very ill . . we go to Seville . . . (*She gets up and goes to* **Maria**.) She is in a coma. (*She sits down by* **Maria**.) Her eyes are closed. (*She closes* **Maria**'s *eyes*.) She is swathed in bandages. (*She* *touches her face.*) Her body is all broken. (*She touches her body.*) For eighteen days . . . she is in a coma. When the bandages are unwrapped her face is criss-crossed with stitch-marks, swollen and bruised. (*She looks at* **Maria**.)

**Maria del Morte** My brother . . . Antonio . . questioned later by a newspaper reporter . . says 'Not for a minute, did we ever doubt that it was my sister!!!'

**Marguerita** We were only allowed to see her for two, three minutes a day!!

**Maria del Morte** Me!!!!

**Marguerita** I was all the time praying that you would live!!!!

**Maria del Morte** *turns away . . . she picks up the newspaper figures . . . reads.*

**Maria del Morte** 'Barbara Avery, seventeen, was convicted today of killing her thirty-nine-day-old daughter Tominka, in an incinerator because she wanted to go to her own birthday party and could not find a baby-sitter. When she could not find a sitter, she dropped the baby into the incinerator and went to the party.'
(*She tears off a cut-out person and holds it in the candle.*) Tominka Avery. (*It smoulders.*)

**Marguerita** Barbara Avery.

**Maria del Morte** *crumples another cut-out figure in her hand.*

**Maria del Morte** When Maria del Amor woke from her coma, after eighteen days, she had lost all memory of who she was.

**Julia** The poor child.

**Maria** She remembered nothing at all?

**Marguerita** She remembered how to eat . . . how to talk . . . she talked a little . . . she could understand . . . read newspapers . .

**Maria** She did not remember . . who her mother was?

**Maria del Morte** No.

**Marguerita** I did my tricks . . . snipping dolls . . . the water . . .
she did not know . . .

**Maria del Morte** No.

**Maria** Heaven. Heaven without angels. She remembers nothing
. . . her growing up always doing, always saying, always being
the wrong *person* . . . She wakes up from a coma and it is like she
has just been born! She is *new*! (*She gets up, looks at* **Julia**.) A new
mother. (*She sits down beside* **Marguerita**.) Maria del Amor. (*She
lies with her head on* **Marguerita***'s lap*.) Yes.

**Marguerita** *strokes her hair.*

**Julia** Maria!

**Maria** Del Amor. It means 'love'.

**Julia** Good! Fine! No daughter then . . . I make meals for
strangers . . . and . . . the dead!!! (*She goes to the dresser . . . gets a
knife*.) Good! Fine! The cord is cut! (*Gets some potatoes*.) I prepare
tortilla de patatas for people off the streets and dead souls down
from heaven! (*She starts to peel potatoes*.)

**Maria del Morte** Meanwhile, seventy miles away, in my home,
in my bed, in my mother's arms . . . the new Maria lives.

**Marguerita** I sleep next to my daughter.
I comfort her as I would a new-born child.
She is so helpless.
I bathe her . . . I dress her . . . I sing to her.

*Sings.*

Fear not the wind
Fear not the storm
I have you here
Safe and warm.

**Maria** Maria Amor Maria

**Maria del Morte** This new-born baby cries . . .

**Maria** Amor, Maria Amor . . .

**Maria del Morte** Ah . . . says everybody . . . the word for love
. . the girl expresses her love for her family!

*The two* **Marias** *look at each other.*
**Maria** *goes to* **Maria del Morte**.

**Maria** You were seventeen.

**Maria del Morte** Yes.

**Maria** I'm seventeen.
*She reaches out and touches* **Maria del Morte**.
You're so cold.

**Maria del Morte** And it was so hot that day.

**Maria** Were you in love?

**Maria del Morte** I don't know.

**Maria** Were you happy?

**Maria del Morte** I don't know.

*They smile.*

**Julia** Maria!

*They both look at her.*

This . . . is dangerous!

*They look back at each other.*

**Maria del Morte** As I convalesce . . . my family begin to notice small changes in me . . .

**Maria** Small changes?

*They both laugh.*

**Julia** I hope when you are a mother, with children . . . you find this as funny!

*She realises what she has said.*

**Both Marias** Tragic!

*They laugh.*

**Marguerita** Quiet!!!

*They become very quiet.*

**Maria del Morte** My family asks the doctors . . . (*She picks up two faces from the newspaper cuttings*) . . Sasebas and Perelada . . . about the small changes in me.

**Marguerita** Why is her hair darker?

**Maria del Morte** (*animates one face or cut-out doll*) It happens, in illness.

**Marguerita** It's coarser . . .

**Maria del Morte** Yes. Illness.

**Marguerita** And her complexion . . . it seems . . . rougher . .

**Maria del Morte** (*animates another*) It's the cortizone injections.

**Marguerita** And . . excuse me . . . someone has painted her toe-nails . .

**Maria del Morte** Eh? . . . no . . .

**Marguerita** And . . she has metal braces attached to her teeth . . . and . . it's a little thing . . but . . . she had a mole on her hip . . . and it's not there now . . .

**Maria del Morte** My family are working class . . . I am the first one from these . . . peasants . . who is going to university . . . the doctors . . educated men . . see only ignorant peasants . . . Look . . why do you care about a little blemish on her hip? . . . These are all side effects from the drugs we are using to get your daughter well! The body responding to trauma . . do you understand, nnnh?

**Marguerita** I'm sorry.

**Maria del Morte** My father asks these questions. Antonio, my brother, asks these questions. My mother asks no questions, does she?

**Marguerita** No.

**Maria del Morte** No. She sings lullabies to me with my small changes! She tends my new-born body!!!

**Marguerita** Maria . . . give me peace!!!

**Maria del Morte** I can't! I'm in hell!!!

*Sings:*

Fear not the wind
Fear not the storm
I have you here
Safe and warm

Fear not the rocks
The ocean deep
I hold you close
Gentle sleep . . .

Singing songs to someone else, comforting someone else . . . My sister . . . Mari Carmen comes down from Figueras to see me . . She looks at me . . . my coarsened darkened hair . . my pug nose . . my braced teeth . . and she shouts . . throughout the hospital . . loud enough to wake the dead . . . seventy miles away in Camas: 'That is not my sister, I don't care what you say. That is not my sister!!!' And what do you say to my sister? What do you say to her?

**Marguerita** I say . . . Mari Carmen, it is your sister. You are overcome . . she is disfigured by the accident . . . the doctors say the cortizone injections . . . they know what they are talking about. It is your sister.

**Maria** *goes to* **Julia**.

**Maria** Mama . . send them away. It scares me.

**Julia** Who are you? Why do you call me Mama? I have no daughter here, do I? My daughter took a new name . . . for *love* . . . she has a new mother . . . in Huelva, does she not? My daughter's room is empty. (*She picks up a newspaper, reads.*) 'Archer Max Hoffman tried to become a modern-day William Tell when he set an apple on his son's head. Unfortunately for his son Wolfgang, the shot missed the apple, and went straight through the ten-year-old boy's head, killing him.' Wolfgang Hoffman. Tell me more of your sick daughter, Señora.

**Marguerita** She calls me and her father by the words 'Father' and 'Mother' instead of Mama and Papa like always before . . With Santiago . . her boyfriend . . . she blows hot and cold . . .

sometimes she lets him kiss her . . other times she shrinks from his touch . . .

**Maria** Mama . . please . . .

**Julia** Please? (*She looks away.*)

**Maria del Morte** (*to* **Maria**) Please . . . (*She touches* **Maria**.) You are so warm . . . lend me your heat so I can rest in peace.

**Maria** How?

**Maria del Morte** Make the journey. We will return.

**Marguerita** We start to make arrangements for plastic surgery . . . to correct this nose . . . change her face to look like our daughter.

**Maria del Morte** They send her to a therapist . . . to speed the recovery of her mind . . . (*She picks up another newspaper picture.*) Enrique Boyer is in his mid-twenties. He has not worked long enough in hospitals to think that all doctors are geniuses . . . all peasants stupid. He has studied psychology at university. He interviews the girl. What is your name?

**Maria** Maria.

**Maria del Morte** (*takes another picture and sits down by* **Maria**) This is the girl he interviewed.

*They both look at the picture.*

Maria del Amor. Imagine how she was. Make the journey. (*She stands up, puts the picture of Enrique Boyer to her face.*) What is your name?

**Maria** (*puts the picture of* **Maria del Amor** *to her face*) Maria del Amor.

**Maria del Morte** Maria del Morte.

**Maria** Maria del Amor.

**Maria del Morte** Maria del Morte.

**Maria** No.

**Maria del Morte** Yes . . . what is your father's surname?

**Maria** del Morte.

**Maria del Morte** What is your mother's surname?

**Maria** del Morte.

**Maria del Morte** What is your name?

**Maria** Maria del Amor.

**Maria del Morte** And where do you live?

**Maria** Number twenty-six, Curro Romero Street, Camas.

**Maria del Morte** Number three, San Clemente Barrio, Huelva.

**Maria** Number twenty-six, Curro Romero Street, Camas.

**Maria del Morte** Number three, San Clemente Barrio, Huelva.

**Maria** No.

**Maria del Morte** Yes. When you leave this office, where do you go to?

**Maria** Number three, San Clemente Barrio, Huelva.

**Maria del Morte** Do you work?

**Maria** I am a student.

**Maria del Morte** Of what?

**Maria** Of beauty therapy.

**Maria del Morte** Of history.

**Maria** Of beauty therapy.

**Maria del Morte** No.

**Maria** Yes. What are the books in your room about?

**Maria** History.

**Maria del Morte** Tell me about your accident.

**Maria** I can't . .

**Maria del Morte** You can. Imagine. Eight-thirty. Hot night.

**Maria** Eight-thirty. Hot night.

**Maria del Morte** Driving to the beach . . .

**Maria** Driving to the beach . . .

**Both** The smell of pine through the open window of the car . . . inside of the car hot.

**Maria del Morte** I'm thinking of my boy-friend.

**Maria** I'm thinking of my girl-friend.

**Both** I go into the curve of a long long bend . . the gravel under the wheels is loose . . the car bucks . . skids . . there's a car coming towards me . . there's a car coming right at me. The wheel won't turn . . . there's a girl coming at me through the windscreen . . . the windscreen's gone blank . . . it's snow, it's ice, it's burning my face, it's cutting my face, it's in my eyes, into my head, it's slicing my brain into pieces of gravel, what is happening? Where am I? Who am I? I am in pieces all over the road!!

**Marguerita** It's eight-thirty.

**Julia** Hot night.

**Marguerita** My daughter is driving to the beach.

**Julia** She said goodbye.

**Marguerita** She's always saying goodbye these days . . .

**Julia** Can't bear to be in the house . .

**Marguerita** Wants to leave you . .

**Julia** Like you wanted to leave her lots of times, when you had to feed her . . wipe her face . . wash her bum . . . play with her . . clean up her table mess . . tidy away her toys again and again and again . . .

**Marguerita** Everywhere else in the world is more exciting than home . .

**Julia** Everyone else in the world is more exciting than you . .

**Marguerita** She drives off . . and you think . . thank God . . a bit of peace from this . . stranger called your daughter . . .

**Julia** This strange girl who despises what you are . .

**Both** The night darkens . . . it's late . . she's always later than she says . . we always have angry words . . it's very late . . the anger turns to fear . . trains collide . . . aeroplanes fall out of the sky . . mad men lurk in the shadows . . cars crash.

**Marguerita** The telephone rings.

**Julia** Who's that at this time of night?

**Marguerita** The police.

**Julia** The hospital.

**Marguerita** Everything you feared.

**Julia** Everything you feared for her.

**Marguerita** Has happened.

**Julia** My daughter.

**Marguerita** The nightmare happens.

**Both**
Fear not the wind
Fear not the storm
I have you here
Safe and warm
Fear not the rocks
The ocean deep
I hold you close
Gently sleep

But in the night, a piper played
Such a tune, of lands unseen
Sunlit forests, mountains high
A winding road, a soaring sky

You dived
You dived

The wind, the storm
The ocean deep
They hold you close
Gently sleep

**Maria del Morte** Two families suffer. In Camas, a mother believes her daughter has lost her life. In Huelva, a mother believes her daughter has lost her memory.

**Marguerita** (*to the two* **Maria**s) Look . . . (*She takes a newspaper and begins tearing it.*) There was once a land with no trees.

**Maria del Morte** *smiles in recognition.*

And it was very hot . . . and the people had no shade. (*She keeps tearing.*) So they went to the wisest old woman of the land and said 'make us a tree'. (*She keeps tearing.*) So she did. (*She starts pulling from the centre of the newspaper and out comes a newspaper palm tree.*) She made them a tree. (*She pulls out some more.*) And it grew and grew and grew. (*It grows and grows and grows.*) Until she had made them a very tall tree. And all the people of the land were happy.

**Maria del Morte** *claps,* **Maria** *does not.*

Here . . (*She gives the tree to* **Maria**.)

**Maria del Morte** The mother in Huelva tries to remind her daughter of the past . . .

**Marguerita** Don't you remember the tree story? Don't you remember the tree? You must remember all the trees I made . .

**Maria del Morte** She begs . . .

**Marguerita** When you were a little girl . . . you were always saying . . .

**Maria del Morte** Make me a tree to sleep under . . .

**Marguerita** Make me a tree to sleep under . .

**Maria del Morte** But the new Maria does not remember the tree . . .

**Maria** I remember another tree . . . (*To* **Julia**.) Do you remember the picnic we had at the Fluvia?

**Julia** In your yellow dress . .

**Maria** That you said I shouldn't wear because I would spoil it . .

**Julia** It was your newest dress . . . for a picnic . .

**Maria** And I cried and cried . . .

**Julia** You shrieked and yelled . . .

**Maria** And finally you said . . .

**Julia** 'God in Heaven . . if it's so important, wear the bloody dress . . . but don't blame me if anything happens to it!!!'

**Maria** And I went to the River Fluvia in my new yellow dress.

**Julia** And I went to the River Fluvia in a stinking temper!

**Maria** And I climbed that tree . . .

**Julia** Overhanging the River Fluvia . .

**Maria** And the branch was slippy and I . .

**Julia** Fell splash into the River Fluvia.

**Maria** And you waded in and fished me out . .

**Julia** So we both got soaked in the River Fluvia!

**Maria** And then Mama . . .

**Julia** And then I looked at you . . your yellow dress . . *khaki* . . with the mud of Fluvia and me . . khaki with the mud of Fluvia . . . and I laughed and laughed and laughed . . .

**Maria** Yes. It's the same thing now, Mama.

**Julia** No.

**Maria** Yes. Let me put on my yellow dress because I'm happy. Let me climb the trees because I am well and happy.

**Julia** And if you *fall*!!!

**Maria** Let me fall!!!

**Julia** Into this stinking disgusting mud which will cover us all . . .

**Maria** Laugh at it! Look at me and laugh . . . because I am happy!!!

**Julia** Listen to me . . . just as I waded into the river and dragged you from the mud of Fluvia . . . so will I wade in and drag you from this mud you wallow in now!!!

**Maria** Aaaaagh! (*She flings the paper tree at* **Julia**.)

**Maria del Morte** What would you have felt, Mother . . . if I had fallen in love with a girl?

**Marguerita** I would have felt as she felt. No mother wants this pain for her daughter.

**Maria del Morte** Or joy either? Enrique Boyer, our therapist, is confused. His patient, Maria, grows physically stronger every day. But what, oh what of her mind? She lives . . in Huelva. (*She draws its position in the dust.*) Her name is Maria del Morte . . . But why, oh why, does she insist on calling herself Maria del Amor . . and giving her address as Camas . . seventy miles away and in a different province? (*She draws its position in the dust.*) Why does a girl from here . . Huelva . . a student of history in Huelva . . know the telephone number of a bar of a beautician's school in Seville? (*Draws in Seville . . studies the puzzle.*) He is puzzled. How can he explain it? He decides to go back to the start, to the accident . . . He searches out the accident report and discovers that it took place at Punta Umbria . . mid-way between Camas and Huelva . . . and discovers that the driver of one car was Maria del Morte, the driver of the other car Maria del Amor who lived in Camas, who now lies buried in the cemetery in Camas. Why has Maria del Morte taken on the details of the dead girl's life? What is your name?

**Maria** Mud.

**Maria del Morte** Where do you live?

**Maria** Here. There. Nowhere.

**Maria del Morte** What is your mother's name?

*No answer from* **Maria**.

**Maria del Morte** What is your father's name?

*No answer from* **Maria**.

**Maria del Morte** Tell me about your accident . . .

**Maria** Leave me alone . . .

**Maria del Morte** Perhaps, thinks Boyer, the girl has overheard the name of Maria del Amor, the address of Maria del Amor, in the confusion after the accident . . . What do you remember of your accident?

**Maria** I was not in this accident!

**Maria del Morte** His theory takes hold.

**Maria** There's a river that flows . . . and . . . you're little . . . and it seems a long way across to the other bank . . so . . you stay on your own side . . . the water up to your ankles . . and then you go in a bit deeper . . to your knees . . and the current flows past you . . pulling your legs . . up to your waist . . up to your chest . . and all the time . . the other bank gets closer . . . until one day . . you're swimming . . and you could do it . . you could reach the other side . . . but by then . . . you can swim . . . and the current's pulling you the other way . . . downstream . . because that way's longer . . . rivers are longer than they are wide . . . and you want to go that way . . not across to the other bank . . .

**Maria del Morte** Enrique Boyer, with his incomplete knowledge, believes that her sanity is flowing away . . .

**Maria** I'll swim.

**Julia** Against the current! It's hard swimming against the current . . .

**Maria** I'm swimming the way I want . . .

**Julia** It's the wrong way!!!

**Maria del Morte** Enrique Boyer reluctantly considers the use of electric shock.

**Maria** Nooooo!!!! (*Takes newspaper and reads.*) 'Two sisters, aged twelve and nineteen, who were kept captive almost all of their lives by their mother, have been freed. The mother, widow Maria Kolb, 48, feared the girls would catch some disease in the outside world. The elder girl, Eva, had spent only six days at primary school, and her sister, Heidi-Marie, had never been to one. The only time they escaped from their home in Bayreuth, Bavaria, was several years ago when their grandmother took them shopping while their mother was out. Police said Mrs Kolb threatened to kill the girls and herself when they went to free them. They found a loaded revolver under a cushion in her living room. The girls looked dazed when taken from their home.'

Looked dazed, looked dazed, looked dazed, Maria Kolb, Eva Kolb, Heidi-Marie Kolb. (*She goes down on her knees and starts writing in the dust.*)

**Maria del Morte** *stands and looks at what she is writing.*

**Maria del Morte** (*reads*) 'To what there is . . . there is . . what there isn't . . to what there is there is what there isn't . . . Enrique Boyer took the girl's scribbling as a plea for help . .

**Maria** Help me . . somebody please help me . . please, please, somebody help me . . .

**Maria del Morte** Enrique Boyer decided to try another tack.

**Marguerita** *takes a small book from her bag, and shows it to* **Julia**.

**Marguerita** Dictionary. I have lately been looking up the meaning of words . .

**Maria del Morte** Boyer came from Catalunya . . in the far north of Spain . .

**Marguerita** I need to know *exactly* what the words mean . . do you understand?

**Maria del Morte** In the opposite corner from Andalucía . . where now he worked . . .

**Marguerita** Words such as love . . . such as death . . such as mother . . . do you know?

**Maria del Morte** But as it happened . . . one of the few people he knew in Andalucía was a doctor from Camas . . .

**Marguerita** When they say 'She is dead' . . . I need to know what that means . . .

**Maria del Morte** The doctor was his friend. It was an extraordinary coincidence.

**Marguerita** Coincidence. (*Starts looking up the word.*) Two girls . . seventeen . . in two cars . . . named Maria . . . meet in the same terrible moment . . (*Reads.*) 'a chance occurrence of events . . . remarkable for apparently being connected . .'

**Maria del Morte** 'It was an extraordinary coincidence' said Boyer . . . Camas is a very small town . . and Spain a very big country!

**Marguerita** What is an accident? Why my daughter? Why her?

**Maria del Morte** Enrique Boyer asks his doctor to come and look at Maria del Morte. Perhaps he will understand why the girl keeps calling 'Amor Amor'. The doctor looks at the girl. He stares. He goes outside. Leans against the wall. 'But this girl is Maria del Amor, San Clemente Barrio, Camas,' he says. This is Maria del Amor!'

**Marguerita** *starts crying.*

**Maria del Morte** The doctor from Camas goes back to the little town . . . he tells Toni Reina . . . the girl's aunt . .

**Marguerita** Like spies . . . traitors . . behind my back . . the doctors plot . .

**Maria del Morte** Toni Reina comes to the clinic at Huelva . . .

**Marguerita** I let her go to the clinic because I thought they were mending her . . .

**Maria del Morte** Toni Reina looks at her niece. 'Do you know who I am?' she asks. Maria del Amor nods calmly.

**Marguerita** How could she *know*?

**Maria del Morte** Toni Reina tells the Mayor of Camas. They start to collect evidence to reclaim the daughter of their town. Frequently, the mayor meets the parents of Maria del Amor on the street . . . he cannot sleep for he is weighted down with his secret.

**Marguerita** No one told me this was happening! Behind my back.

**Maria del Morte** Then the mayor tells the parents of Maria del Amor. It is arranged for the father to see Maria del Amor in the Huelva clinic.

**Marguerita** Still nobody tells us!

**Maria del Morte** The father looks at the girl. He is in anguish. He wants to shout . . . to take her in his arms . . to hold her safe. Maria del Amor registers no surprise at seeing her father. She smiles. She puts her finger to her lips and says 'Shhh. Otherwise they'll leave me here.'

**Marguerita** Shhh. Otherwise they'll leave me here.

**Maria del Morte** Maria del Amor's father goes to the police to demand the return of his daughter. What did this family want with his daughter? How could they not know that Maria del Amor was not their child?

**Marguerita** All this time . . I am letting her go to the clinic, believing they are making her well. My husband is called in. He is shown photograph albums of the girl. He tells my son Antonio . . . 'It's not your sister . . . it's someone else . . . I have seen an album full of photographs of the girl' . . It all becomes clear to them . . all the doubts . . . the painted toe-nails . . . the missing mark on her thigh . . so. So . . my family do not have the courage to tell me the truth . . . they say Maria is needed for urgent tests . . and my husband escorts her round the corner . . where her father waits with two police officers. And on August the first . . . for the second time . . my daughter is taken away from me forever.

*There is silence.*

**Julia** How could you not know that she was not yours?

*No answer.*

**Marguerita** *takes a newspaper and starts to tear it.*

**Julia** For seventeen years you held this girl . . you fed her at your breast . . . you looked with wonder on her every day . . knowing she was yours . . . when she fell down . . you kissed her face and rubbed her knee and saw that she was better . . . when she cried

. . *you* hurt . . . when she screamed . . . you felt the pain in *your* heart . . . when she fell into danger . . . *you* were gripped at the throat with fear . . . How could you not know that she was not your child???

**Marguerita** *says nothing. She continues tearing her newspaper.*

And somewhere . . . all this time . . . was a mother . . . just like you . . . feeling as you felt . . . sitting in a dark room . . lit by one lamp . . . staring into the night . . thinking no thought but this . . . my daughter is dead . . . I cannot understand it . . . my daughter is dead! How could you do it? (*She goes to* **Maria**.) Maria . . . whatever you are . . . whatever I am . . I know one thing . . . you are my daughter . . . and I love you more than life. Let us go into the house and I will block your door shut with a chair so that ghosts cannot come and take you.

**Maria** Mama. No. What you fear for me can't be held by a chair against a door. A thousand chairs against a thousand doors will not keep it out. Something has come and taken me. The ghosts are here.

**Maria del Morte** My body was dug up and brought back from Camas to Huelva. I was returned to my family. My parents were too upset to identify me. They asked my brother, Antonio to look at me . . . see that it was me. After two months in the coffin . . my looks had gone. I had decomposed badly. My skin had blackened. The smell was nauseous. But Antonio could recognise me instantly. 'It was horrible,' he says. 'When I see a photograph of my sister now, or when I talk about her, the image of her all black inside the coffin comes back to me. I can't get rid of it.' He does not sleep now . . . for I can come through a thousand doors. (*She smiles*.) The one advantage of being dead. I may visit where I please . . . whenever I please . . .

*Sings.*

A thousand chairs
Against a thousand doors
A thousand doors
In a thousand walls

Will not keep me away
I will come to you.

A thousand keys
Turned in a thousand locks
A thousand links
In a thousand chains
Will not keep me away
I will come to you . . .

**Maria** *stands and watches* **Marguerita** *tearing her paper.*

**Maria** Señora, what are you doing?

**Marguerita** Tearing newspaper.

**Maria** Señora . . . how could you not know that it was not your daughter?

**Marguerita** How could I not know.
This is a question I have been asked a thousand times . . .
How could I not know?
Asked by the police . . .
How could I not know?
Asked by the neighbours . . .
How could I not know?
Asked by my children . . .
How could I not know?
Asked by the newspapers . . . every newspaper in all of Spain . . .
Señora . . . but how . . . excuse me . . a few words . . . for our readers . . . for the public . . . how could you not know that this girl was not your daughter?

**Maria del Morte** I cannot rest . . . I cannot sleep . . . I cannot lie down in my blackened, stinking, decomposing body in the graveyard in Huelva . . until my mind is at peace . . . Mother . . . how could you not know that it wasn't me???

**Marguerita** *touches her daughter's face.*
**Maria del Morte** *does nothing.*

**Marguerita** In Camas . . . a daughter believed dead, was returned to her mother. The newspapers are filled with stories of the girl's reunion with her parents. A television programme

names her 'Andalucían of The Year'. Camino, the matador,
dedicates the killing of a bull to her in the Seville bull ring. A film
company want to make a film version of her story. There is much
rejoicing . . that a daughter, believed dead, was returned to her
mother.

**Maria del Morte** On All Soul's Day . . Maria . . the living
Maria . . asks her parents to take her to see her crypt in Camas
cemetery. The crypt in which my body lay for two months. She
said 'I want to discover something of that other world.' She stood
before her empty tomb and laughed. (*To* **Maria**.) Wouldn't you?

**Maria** Yes.

**Maria del Morte** Glad to be alive.

**Maria** Yes.

**Marguerita** A daughter returned from the dead. Yes, I would
laugh too. If I could have my daughter returned from the dead
. . . I would do anything . . I would care for her as a new-born
baby . . . I would sleep next to her and comfort her . . .
I would take the paint off her toe-nails. I would say 'there was no
mark on her thigh . . . I would have her nose changed by plastic
surgery . . . I would send volt after volt through her brain until
she *was* my Maria!!!

*She pulls out the newspaper. It is a long, long ladder.*

**Julia** Oh God!

**Marguerita** My daughter was dead . . . I tried to build a ladder
so I could climb to hell and get her . . . How could I not know
that this Maria was not mine? I *knew*! I knew the first day it
wasn't my daughter. How could I not? (*Pause*.) But . . . I couldn't
bring myself to let her go.

*There is complete silence.*

**Maria** What if . . . the electric shock treatment had . . . had
worked . . . what if she . . . the girl . . . had never remembered
who she really was?

**Marguerita** I don't know. I was found out. It is in all the
newspapers. I am infamous.

**Maria del Morte** Mama. It is time you went home. There is a family there who loves you. There is a grave to tend in Huelva in which lies the body of your daughter. Go home . . . Let the newspapers write that there lives a mother who loved her daughter so much. The one advantage of a dead daughter is that she can visit where she pleases . . when she pleases . . . I will come through a thousand doors to you to the end of your life. And then, perhaps, you will come to me. (*She goes.*)

*The two women and the girl sit.*

**Maria** It's cold.

**Julia** The sun's gone. (*She shivers.*) Señora . . . it's time I made supper . . come in and sit by the cooker while I make some nice hot tortillas de patatas . . mmm?

**Marguerita** I must go home.

**Julia** Eat first.

**Marguerita** I'm not hungry.

**Maria** I am.

**Marguerita** Good. Eat it up. Every scrap.

*She stands, collects her bag and possessions.*

**Marguerita** Eating her supper now . . is a girl also called Maria. Her broken ankle is mended, the scars on her face have healed, her memory has returned. She remembers the accident. She remembers nothing of the time she spent with me. I am very happy about this. I'm not her mother, you see. I lay my hand upon the forehead of this house. Let it be free of pain. (*She goes.*)

*Pause.*

**Julia** Well. Tortilla de patatas.

**Maria** Mmm . . . yes . .

**Julia** Tomato salad . . .

**Maria** Oh . . yes . .

**Julia** And . . . a little chorizo!

**Maria** And a lot of chorizo!

**Julia** Right then! (*She gets up with her peeled potatoes, half-way to the house, she stops.*) Did that . . . just then . .

**Maria** No! Don't say . . . . Pretend we read it in the newspapers.

**Julia** Right. Right then. (*She goes a quarter of the way to the house. She stops.*) After supper . . .

**Maria** What?

**Julia** You're not going out, I suppose . . .

**Maria** I don't know.

**Julia** It'll be late . .

**Maria** Not that late.

**Julia** But you won't be going out . .

**Maria** I might.

**Julia** I don't think you should, not tonight.

**Maria** Well . . . I might not. I'll see.

**Julia** You'll see.

**Maria** Probably not. I'll see.

**Julia** Well after tortilla and tomato salad and chorizo . . I'd just be too full to move!

**Maria** Mmm . . I know . . .

*She stretches on a bench, as if there for life.*

**Julia** Right! Tortilla de patatas.

*Goes into the house singing . . .*

Fear not the wind
Fear not the storm
I have you here
Safe and warm

**Maria** *listens to her mother singing.*

**Maria** Here's what I'm going to do tonight. After supper . . . I'm going to put on my . . . blue dress . . yes . . . and I'll go to . . . to Philipe's because . . because they play good music . . . and

everybody'll be there . . and . . . Paula . . . she'll be there . . .
and we'll all have a good time . . . we'll dance with the boys . . .
Pepe . . . and Juan-Carlos . . . and Michelito . . and then . . .
we'll get in Paula's car . . . just Paula and me . . . and we'll drive
with the windows open so we can smell the pine . . . through the
woods . . by the *twisty* road . . down to the beach for a swim. And
when we're in the water . . . I might, I just might get hold of
Paula . . . and kiss her dead on the lips! Yes!

*As she makes up she sings.*

A thousand chairs
Against a thousand doors
A thousand doors
In a thousand walls
Will not keep me away
I will come to you.

A thousand keys
Turned in a thousand locks
A thousand links
In a thousand chains
Will not keep me away
I will come to you

**Julia** (*from within the house*) Maria!

**Maria** What?

**Julia** Supper!

**Maria** *goes into the house.*

Wicked

**Wicked** was first performed by Clean Break Theatre Company at the Oval House, London on 14 February 1990 with the following cast:

**Bailey One**
**Banshee**
**Screw Lou**          Sue Rossiter
**Tina**

**Evvie**
**Bailey Two**
**Screw Sue**          Caroline S Sharp
**Kim**

**Zombie**
**Screw Moo**
**Terry**              Collette Johnson
**Rosie**
**Bailey Three**


*Directed by* Joan Ann Maynard
*Musical Director* Laka Daisical
*Designer* Galia Shaw
*Lighting Design* Paul J Need
*Magic Consultancy and illusion* Fay Presto

Scene One

## The Wonderful World of Show Business

*The space has been bare. Now it is occupied by a collection of suitcases, trunks, containers, boxes which form a pile. All of them are locked and padlocked. A seedy, theatrical feel.*

**Girlie**, *the Stage Manager, brings on and adds to the pile. She checks the sound and lights. She carries the keys to everything.*

**Bailey One**, *a man, oversees and checks on* **Girlie**'s *progress. He stands in the spotlights, adjusts the boxes. He sits at the keyboard, raises his hands and waits.* **Girlie** *comes over and unlocks the keyboard. He waits as she returns to her sound and lights.*

**Bailey** Ready?

**Girlie** *nods.*

**Bailey** *turns to the audience with a spectacular smile.*

Ladies and Gentlemen, everywhere, anywhere . . . . .
Welcome to My World!!!

**Girlie** *brings up a bright spot on* **Bailey One**. *He plays and sings.*

*Song: Always There*

**Bailey One**
Hey there, little girl
Feeling small?
I'll be your white knight
Brave, strong and tall.

Hey there, little girl
Feeling weak?
I'll be your partner
We'll dance cheek to cheek.

Like Ginger Rogers and Fred Astaire
Like a warm cuddly teddy bear
Like a blanket from Mothercare
I'll be
There for you
Like Lancelot for Guinevere
Like Rudolph the red-nosed reindeer
Like Cordelia for poor old King Lear
I'll be
There for you
Always there

Like an empty sunbed on a crowded beach
Like a life belt your drowning arms can reach
Like a thirst-quenching ripe juicy peach
I'll be
There for you
Like a camel in the Sahara sand
Like an injection of monkey gland
Like a soothing cream when you're over-tanned
I'll be
There for you
Always there

Like a Gideon bible in a hotel room
Like lighting-up time in the winter gloom
Like the AA when your car won't vroom
I'll be
There for you
Like the last bus on a rainy night
Like TCP on an insect bite
Like smelling salts when you've had a fright
I'll be
There for you
Always there

Like Paris in the spring
Like the glad tidings the angels bring
Like Dana and all kinds of everything
I'll be there for you

Like a father for his little daughter
Like a helpful railway porter
Like a bridge over troubled water
I'll be
There for you
Always there

Always there for you darling

I'm your man

For you
Always there

Always been an impresario, a showman, a maker of scenes, I run
the show . . . .

*Music underscores his speech.*

In the beginning there was nothing
'Start it with a big bang', I said

**Girlie** *sounds a big bang.*

'Let there be light,' I said

**Girlie** *lights stars.*

'Let there be a world to dance in,' I said

*He dances.*

'Let there be a man to mess it up and a woman to clean it up,' I
said. And lo, you've got a show, eh Girlie? I'm the beast of the
earth, I'm the wingéd fowl, I'm everything that creepeth upon
the earth, every creeping thing I am and what a show I've got for
you tonight!!! Noisier than the Tower of Babel, dirtier than
Sodom and Gomorrah, sneakier than the wooden horse of Troy,
bloodier than the bloodiest wars of this wicked wild wonderful
world, have I for you tonight. What is it? What makes the saliva
slurp? What clammies the clap equipment? What creams the
jeans? I'll tell you, you rows of eyes, you folds of arms, you bench
of bums . . . I've done shows of astonishing beauty. I've done
acts of sublime love. I've shown the wonders of the world in all
their astonishing and infinite variety. I've shown a seed meet an

egg, a coupling of energetic juices and the miracle of miracles: a
birth, a perfect birth. Awwwwwwwwwwwwwwwh! Is that what
you want? An infant perfect in all its limbs and senses? Not
quite. We're all standing about the bed. The mother's straining,
screaming . . . We're all standing about the bed . . . The baby's
coming . . . it's coming . . it's coming feet first! One little foot . .
two little feet . . three little feet . . . now *that's* unusual! It keeps
coming . . it's got no arms . . just hands sticking straight out
from the shoulders! Here comes its head . . . And its other head
. . . It's a three-legged, no-armed, two-headed baby. Now there's
a thing! I'm impresario, I'm showman, I run the show, I take it,
I'm in the business of freaks. 'Today a normal healthy child was
born to an ordinary woman.' Wouldn't make the news, would it?
But a freak . . a disaster . . a different . . . an out . . an odd . . . a
strange . . . a fright . . . Here is the News!!!! Have I got a show
for you tonight!!!

*He bangs the cases.*

What's the freakiest you can get?
In here!

*Bangs the boxes.*

What's the weirdest you could want?

*Bangs the containers.*

In here, friends!
Where's the shockingest show?

*Taps a small box.*

Here! Is it the escaping escapologist? Is it the vanishing
magician? Is it the gigantic giant? The minute midget? The
strong man? The bearded lady? Panama! Homburg! Trilby! Old
Hat hahahaaaaaaa! Lucia Zarate, 1863 to 1889, was the shorter
of two sisters who formed a circus act, called 'The Mexican
Midgets'. Lucia measured 1 foot 8 inches. She weighted 4.7 lbs at
the age of seventeen. We can do better than that. Jane Bunford,
1895 to 1922, born at Bartley Green, England, Jane stood 7 feet,
7 inches tall, though she would have measured 7ft 11 inches had
it not been for a curvature of the spine. She attained the greatest

scientifically verified height for a woman, and she grew her hair to a record length of 8 feet. We can do better than that. Frank Lentini, The King Of Freaks, was the result of non-separating triplets. He had three legs, two sets of genitals, four feet and sixteen toes. He could use the third leg, which grew out of the base of his spine, as a stool. In his circus act, he could kick a football the length of the sideshow tent. We can do we can do so much better than that. Girlie . . . unlock . . . this one.

**Girlie** *goes to a case and starts unlocking it.*

Hey there, little girl
Feeling small?
I'll be your white knight
Brave, strong and tall.

Hey there, little girl
Feeling weak?
I'll be your partner
We'll dance cheek to cheek.

**Girlie** *stands by the case, which is now unlocked.*

Okay?

*She nods.*

Okay.

*She goes back to her place.*

Okay. Let's see what we've got in the box tonight!

*The music dies away.* **Bailey One** *and* **Girlie** *wait.*


Scene Two

**The Art of Producing Vocal Sounds That Appear To Come From Another Source**

*We watch the case for some time. Nothing happens.* **Bailey One** *looks at* **Girlie**, **Girlie** *looks at* **Bailey One**. *They both look at the case. Nothing happens. They both look at the audience. They look back at the* *box. Nothing happens. They look back at the audience. Nothing happens. This continues until it is unbearable. Finally . . .*

**Bailey One** (*to himself*) Haaaaaah! (*A sigh. To audience.*) Haaaaaaaah! (*A big sigh.*) (*To* **Girlie**.) Haaaaaaaaaaaah! (*A bigger, disappointed sigh. Gets up and walks over to the case. To* **Girlie**.) Haaaaaaaaaaaaaaaaaaaaaaah! (*A very disappointed sigh. He lifts up the lid of the case. To* **Girlie**.) Haaah! (*To audience.*) Haaaaaaah! (*He goes back to his place.*)

*We watch the open case for some time. Nothing happens.* **Bailey One** *looks at* **Girlie**, **Girlie** *looks at* **Bailey One**. *They both look at the case. Nothing happens. They both look at the audience. They look back at the case. Nothing happens. They look back at the audience. Nothing happens. This continues until it is unbearable. Finally . . .*

(*To himself.*) Haaaah! (*To audience.*) Haaaah! (*To* **Girlie**.) Haaaaaah! (*Gets up and walks back to the case.*) Haaaaaaaaaaaah! (*He stands beside the case.*) Do we have a problem in there, do we? Mmm? Is there a problem, is there? (*He looks down into the case. From the box we hear a voice (**Evvie**) whispering. We can hear the sound but not the content.*)

**Evvie** I'm tired.

**Bailey One** You're tired? I'm tired. They're tired.

**Evvie** I've got a headache.

**Bailey One** You've got a headache? I've got a headache! We've all got a headache!

**Evvie** I'm scared.

**Bailey One** You're scared??? I'm scared . . they're scared . . . we're all scared!!!

**Evvie** I just don't want to come out.

**Bailey One** Well . . that's just too bad . . . I've done the intro . . given you a *hell* of an intro!!! . . . everybody's sitting out here with bated breath. Now get out here or I'll pull your arms off!

**Evvie** No.

**Bailey One** Yes.

**Evvie** No.

**Bailey One** Yes!

**Evvie** No.

**Bailey One** Yes! Right! I'm going to come in and get you out!

**Evvie** Oh no you're not!

**Bailey One** Oh yes I am!

**Evvie** Oh no you're not!

**Bailey One** Oh yes I am!

*He reaches in the case and pulls out an arm, which he hangs over the side. He turns away . . it pulls back in the box.*

Right . . now . . . (*Turns back.*) . . . Haaah! (*Sigh.*)

*He reaches in again takes out other arm, hangs it over the side. Turns away . . it pulls back in again.*

Right . . . now . . . (*Turns back.*) . . . Haaaaah!

*He reaches in, pulls out the head . . . it pulls back in, pulling him with it. Then follows a fierce battle, in and out of the case, which* **Bailey One** *finally wins, with the character from the case flopped face down on the floor in front.* **Bailey One** *pants, bent over with a stitch, exhausted by the battle.*

Whooooh! . . . . aaagh! . . . . oof! . . . . aaagh . . . . oof . . . . . phoooh . . . . ow . . . . oooh . . . . phooh . . . phew . . (*Etc.*)

*Meanwhile the character from the case is speaking, its face pressed into the floor.*

**Evvie** I'm not happy . . . . I'm not happy at all . . . . oh misery . . . . oh woe . . . woe . . . woe . . . waaaaaaaaaaaaah! Me bloody nose is bloody running, there's going to be snot all over the bloody floor and all over my bloody face! Waaaaaaaaaaaaaaah!

**Bailey One** Shut up!

*The crying stops abruptly. Silence. Then there are intermittent grunts and sniffs.*

**Evvie** Umnnngh! Unh! Mfffh! Nughhhh! Sniff!

**Bailey One** Right!

*He takes a chair, places it. With enormous effort he manœuvres* **Evvie** *up and sits on the chair with her on his knee.*

Ladies and gentlemen . . . my first exhibit!

*His first exhibit is a mess. She is sniffing and gulping. He takes out a handkerchief, holds it to her nose. She blows loudly. He wipes.*

Okay?

**Evvie** Okay.

*She hiccups. She hiccups again. And again.*

**Bailey One** (*to* **Girlie**) Could I have a glass of water?

**Girlie** *brings him some water. He drinks it.* **Evvie**'s *hiccups stop.*

Okay?

**Evvie** Okay.

**Girlie** *takes glass away.*

**Bailey One** Ladies and gentlemen, my first exhibit.

*We look at his first exhibit:* **Evvie**, *half woman, half ventriloquist's dummy.*

Tell the ladies and gentlemen your name . . .

**Evvie** Margaret Thatcher.

**Bailey One** Tell the ladies and gentlemen your name.

**Evvie** Krystal Carrington.

**Bailey One** I said tell the ladies and gentlemen your name!

**Evvie** Dummy.

**Bailey One** Thank you. And tell the ladies and gentlemen what's special about you, Dummy.

**Evvie** I'm naughty.

**Bailey One** What else?

**Evvie** I'm bad.

**Bailey One** What else?

**Evvie** I'm wicked.

**Bailey One** What else?

**Evvie** I've been in prison.

**Bailey One** You've been in prison?

**Evvie** Yes.

**Bailey One** What were you in prison for?

**Evvie** Stealing.

**Bailey One** What did you steal?

**Evvie** A sweater and two skirts.

**Bailey One** Why did you steal a sweater and two skirts?

**Evvie** I wanted a sweater and two skirts.

**Bailey One** What else?

**Evvie** A packet of frozen lasagne, some granary bread and a tin of Pal.

**Bailey One** Why did you steal those?

**Evvie** I was hungry.

**Bailey One** Tin of Pal?

**Evvie** I had a dog.

**Bailey One** What else?

**Evvie** A bottle of whiskey.

**Bailey One** Why did you steal a bottle of whiskey?

**Evvie** My dog drinks whiskey.

**Bailey One** What?

**Evvie** I like whiskey.

**Bailey One** Do you like stealing?

**Evvie** No.

**Bailey One** Do you like stealing?

**Evvie** No.

**Bailey One** Do you like stealing?

**Evvie** I love it.

**Bailey One** You're a very bad girl.

**Evvie** Yes.

**Bailey One** A very bad, wicked girl.

**Evvie** Yes.

**Bailey One** A very bad, wicked, sinful girl.

**Evvie** Yes. And a brilliant thief!

**Bailey One** Shut up!

**Evvie** Yes.

*She flops to her knees.*

**Bailey One** What are you doing?

**Evvie** I'm praying for forgiveness.

**Bailey One** That's right.

**Evvie** For my most grievous sins.

**Bailey One** That's good.

**Evvie** O lord, when thou callest me before thee, I want thee to take a sweater and two skirts, a packet of frozen lasagne, a tin of Pal and a bottle of whiskey into consideration . .

**Bailey One** That's very good.

**Evvie** Also the Christmas pudding, the potatoes and the Jammy Dodgers from Tescos . . . the cheddar cheese, the Savoury Thins and the avocados from Safeways . . . the check winter coat from Marks and Spencer's . . . the green sweatshirt from Mr Byrite and the sweatpants . . . the vodka, the gin, the tequila from Victoria Wines . . . also the dog basket from Perfect Pets . .

**Bailey One** You're showing me up.

**Evvie** And my knees are getting sore.

**Bailey One** *lifts her back on his lap.*

**Bailey One** No wonder you were sent to prison.

**Evvie** No wonder.

**Bailey One** You're a menace to society.

**Evvie** To society . . . a menace.

**Bailey One** And you a woman.

**Evvie** And me a woman. And a dog owner.

**Bailey One** And a dog . . . shut up!

**Evvie** Shut up.

**Bailey One** Yes, ladies and gentlemen . . . what we've got for you here tonight . . . is that perversion, that deviation, that abhorrent straying from the straight and narrow path of feminine goodness and truth . . . A CRIMINAL WOMAN!

**Evvie** Where?

*She looks to her left and her right.*

**Bailey One** Here!

**Evvie** (*beads* **Girlie**) There?

**Bailey One** No!

**Evvie** (*beads audience*) Out there?

*She gets up and starts walking towards them, dragging* **Bailey** *in her wake.*

**Bailey One** No!

**Evvie** (*makes a beeline for somebody in the audience*) Is it her, is she one, is she?

**Bailey One** No, no, no, no No!!!!

*He drags* **Evvie** *back to the chair. Sits her in it. Takes out his handkerchief and wipes his forehead. Spots something nasty in it from when* **Evvie** *blew her nose. He examines it, grimaces, puts it away.*

It's you.

**Evvie** It's me?

**Bailey One** It's you.

**Evvie** I'm a . . .

**Bailey One** Criminal Woman. Yes.

**Evvie** And I'm a . . .

**Bailey One** Perversion. Yes.

**Evvie** And a . . .

**Bailey One** Deviation . . yes.

**Evvie** And a . . .

**Bailey One** And an abhorrent straying from the straight and narrow path of feminine goodness and truth, yes.

**Evvie** (*she whistles*) Shriewwwwh! Strewth! (*She thinks.*) Who says?

**Bailey One** I say.

**Evvie** (*to* **Girlie** *smugly*) I'm a Criminal Woman . . he says.

**Bailey One** It's nothing to be proud of.

**Evvie** No. (*To audience, smugly.*) . . I'm a Criminal Woman . . (*She whistles.*) Shriewwwh!

**Bailey One** Shut up.

**Evvie** I'm an outlaw.

**Bailey One** You're a disgrace.

**Evvie** I'm wild.

**Bailey One** You're bad.

**Evvie** I'm Robin Hood.

**Bailey One** You're no bleeding good!

**Evvie** Blaaaah!!!

**Bailey One** Careful . . .

**Evvie** Bleeaaaaaaaah . . . horrid suit . .

**Bailey One** Watch it!

**Evvie** Look at the hair cut!

**Bailey One** I'm warning you . . .

**Evvie** A face only a mother could love . .

**Bailey One** DO YOU WANT TO GO BACK IN THE
BOX????

**Evvie** NO!!!!!!

**Bailey One** Well, behave yourself then.

**Evvie** Yes.

**Bailey One** Or it's the four walls . .

**Evvie** Yes.

**Bailey One** And the locks . . .

**Evvie** Yes.

**Bailey One** And the dark . . .

**Evvie** Umphhh (*She swallows.*)

**Bailey One** All right. Now . . . do your piece for the ladies and
gentlemen.

**Evvie** My piece. Yes.

**Bailey One** Sit up. Look smart.

**Evvie** Yes.

**Bailey One** Like a nice girl.

**Evvie** My piece. (*She clears her throat and folds her hands on her lap.*)
My piece. It's called 'I've Always Been a Naughty Girl' and it's
auto-gri.bath.ic . . .

**Bailey One** Autobiographical . . . .

**Evvie** Autogriobathical. Yes.

I've always been a naughty girl
Right from my mother's knee
I'd climb into her lap and sit
And then I'd have a pee . . .

**Bailey**'s *eyes narrow with suspicion.*

nut, and I'd eat it
And then I'd scoff the lot
Saying 'you see this on my upper lip
You think it's water but it's snot'

**Bailey**'s *eyes narrow again.*

My mother she would rock me
And kiss me a little bit
Then undo the buttons on her dress
And say 'do you like tit . . .'

**Bailey** *looks alert, suspicious.*

tle-tattle, because I don't
I'd rather do some cooking
Or have a drink with a dear dear friend
And get around to fucking

**Bailey** What????

**Evvie**
Fuchien  . . it's a region in China
Where the Emperors used to hunt
But the thing I really prefer to do
Is to shout I love my cunt . . .

**Bailey One** RIGHT, THAT'S IT, I'M NOT HAVING IT!!!

*He stands.*

**Evvie**
ry . . . my country it is of thee
England, merry England
Home of the brave and the free!

**Bailey One** I'm not having women talking like this in *my* show!!! Back in the box!

**Evvie** No!!!!

**Bailey One** *starts lifting her and dragging her back to the case.*

I was just having fun . . . not the box . . . not back in there . . .

*He starts thrusting her into the case.*

Not the dark!!!

*Keeps pushing her in.* **Evvie** *puts up a spirited fight.*

No no no no no no!!!

*He gets all of her in and shuts down the lid. She puts her head out.*

Poooooo!

*He crams her head down, closes the lid and sits on it. There is a tremendous banging from within the case.*

**Bailey One** Girlie! Keys!

**Girlie** *comes with the keys. She locks the case.*

Okay. Chair! (**Bailey One** *signals to* **Girlie** *to take chair.*)

**Girlie** *returns to her place.* **Bailey One** *gets off the case. The banging continues, becomes sporadic, stops.*

Tut tut tut! Some girls, some naughty girls have to be locked up for their own good!

There was a little girl
And she had a little curl
Right in the middle of her forehead
And when she was good
She was very very good
And when she was bad . . . .
She was punished!

*He knocks on the lid of the case. He listens. There is no answer. He walks back to his place. Halfway there, we hear one ominous knock.*

Scene Three

**Someone Quiet**

**Bailey One** Too noisy! Too naughty! Get me someone quiet.

**Girlie** *gets up, goes to the stack of cases. From another of the openings, she unlocks a door. She opens it and stands aside. Mist issues from the entrance. There is a weird half-light. There is a sound of distant drumming. From the door, slowly, shuffling, comes a human figure. It is a woman with an expressionless face and dead, dead eyes. She stands in front of the door.*

**Zombie** Haiti, Haiti, an island in the West Indies. People of Haiti fear to be out in a lonely place at night. They are afraid, they are afraid that they might see, that they might see a figure come slowly toward them, a gaunt human figure with staring eyes, moving with stiff, slow, shuffle.

A Zombie

Zombie, Zombie, a person whose soul was stolen by evil witch who then seemed to die. We are afraid, we are afraid for when they buried it the witch dig up the body, bring it back to life as slave, a gaunt human figure with staring eyes moving with stiff, slow, shuffle.

A Zombie

Zombie, Zombie, could see and move, but could not think for itself. We are afraid, we are afraid it can only do the bidding of its master, who might put it to endless work, or far worse, send it out at night to rob and murder. A gaunt figure, with staring eyes, moving with stiff, slow, shuffle . . . . .

*The **Zombie** stands by **Girlie**. Both are very still and quiet.*

**Bailey One** (*in terrified whisper*) I said get someone quiet . . but not *this* quiet!!! Stupid girl, Girlie!!!

**Girlie** *bows her head.*

What's that on its collar?

*On its collar, pinned, is an official-looking envelope.*

Is it an envelope?

**Girlie** *nods*.

Well get it, get it.

**Girlie** *unpins the envelope. The* **Zombie** *does not move.*

Bring it here . . it's probably for me

**Girlie** *brings it.*

I like to read all the letters these girls send . . just check they're
not *up* to any monkey business . . . (*He opens the envelope, reads.*)
'Dear . . .
Yesterday I was walking up the stairs to my landing and
suddenly I had a terrible desire to scream. I thought, I must stop
now and scream – let it all come out. But then, as I shook on the
verge of action, I thought, what will happen to me if I do let go?
Of course I shall be dragged away. The scream stays inside. You
have to cut off from the outside and concentrate on being inside.
Lots of love . . . A Zombie from Haiti'?

I don't think so. (*He tears up the letter.*) Don't want this sort of
rubbish getting out. Someone whose soul has been stolen?
Someone whose body has been dug up? Someone who can see
and move, but not think for themself? Let's see.

*He goes to the* **Zombie**.

Walk.

*She does.*

Stop.

*She does.*

Turn round.

*She does.*

Walk.

*She does.*

Stop.

*She does.*

Turn round.

*She does.*

Very good.
My little dog, my little horse, my little empty body, kneel down.

*She does. He takes a duster from his pocket, presents it to her.*

Dust.

*She does.*

**Girlie** *watches.*

Perfect prison material. Obedient. Quiet. Hardworking.

*He gets hold of* **Girlie***, puts his finger to his lips. They tiptoe behind the stack of cases. The* **Zombie** *dusts. She dusts towards* **Girlie***'s place. She dusts the lighting deck. She is bathed in light. She looks up. Her eyes become less dead. She sees the keyboard. Walks over to it. Her walk less of a shuffle. She dusts the keyboard. Music plays. She looks around at where she is. She sings.*

*Song: Landlocked Sea*

**Zombie**
Outside
A grey desert
All is dry
Outside
A parched land,
Inside I cry

Inside
A tear rolls down my face
At my feet, a pool
My tears, join other tears
Soon a whirling pool
Inside
A whirling pool

Outside
All is dry

Inside
The whirling pool is full
Breaks its banks, a stream

My tears, join other tears
Soon a racing stream
Inside
A racing stream

Outside
A parched land

Inside
The racing stream flows fast
Wide and deep, a sea
My tears join other tears
Soon a salty sea
Inside
A salty sea

Outside
All is dry

Inside
A tear rolls down my face
Outside all is dry
My seas join other seas
Soon a mighty flood
Outside
A mighty flood

*She finishes singing, dusts the music to silence. Returns to the lighting board, dusts the lights to earlier state. Returns to her position, kneeling on the floor dusting. She is doing this when* **Bailey Two** *comes onstage with* **Girlie**. **Bailey Two** *is wearing the same suit as* **Bailey One** *but is now played by another actor.*

**Bailey Two** You see . . . ??? Obedient, good, hardworking. Stop.

*She stops.*

Give me that.

*She gives him the duster. He shows* **Girlie** *the dirt on the duster.*

Look at that . . . . dirty, dusty and dry in here, eh? Stand up.

*She stands up.*

If everybody served their time here like you, little darling, the place would be a much better place, eh?

*She stares dully at him.*

Look at that . . . nothing in there . . . nothing at all . . . like looking down into a deep, dark, empty drain. Turn around.

*She turns around.*

Walk back in.

*She walks back in.*

Close the door.

**Girlie** *closes the door. She takes out her keys and locks door.*

Hardly worth locking. Too quiet to cause any trouble.

**Girlie** *puts away her keys. Returns to her place.*


Scene Four

**The Banshee**

**Bailey Two** Another one, I think. That does more than dust.

*He goes to the cases.*

Up the ladder
Down the ladder
Dibdib tation
How many crims
Get locked in the station
I say this one here!

*He has been touching different cases. Dibs one out.*

Girlie!

*She comes to unlock it.*

Hello . . . there's a label on here . .

*He reads the label.*

. . . . Banshee . . . Ireland . . . What's a Banshee?

*The lid of the box bursts open.*

**Banshee** (*from within box*) . . . It was a dark night in Ireland.

*The stage is plunged into darkness.*

Ragged clouds drifted across a moonless sky. Wind rippled the tall grass in the meadows.

*Sound of wind.*

Suddenly, a frightful sound was heard. It began as a low moan,

*Low moan.*

rising into a long wailing shriek,

*Long wailing shriek.*

that slowly faded into a sob.

*Fades into a sob.*

It was the wail of a Banshee . . . and it meant that death was coming for someone!

**Bailey Two** (*frightened whisper*) . . . What's happened to the lights, the lights are off, it's bloody dark in here!

**Banshee** A banshee was heard, and perhaps seen, only when someone was soon to die, it appeared as a beautiful weeping woman in a long green gown and a grey cloak. Her eyes were red from weeping, and as she wailed, she tore her hair in grief.

*The lights come up slowly. There is a sound of weeping and wailing from the box. Every now and then a bit of hair is thrown out.*

**Bailey Two** I think maybe we'll have something from one of the other boxes . . . Aaagh!

*A piece of paper is thrown out. He picks it up, looks at it in bafflement.*

It's a limerick! (*Reads.*) . . .
There was a young woman called Bowers
Who was locked up for twenty-three hours

She said 'frankly I preferred
To be shot and interred
In a grave with a lot of nice flowers'.

*Another piece of paper is thrown out, he picks it up.*

It's another limerick!!! (*Reads.*) . . .
There was a young woman called Wanger
Who experienced uncontrollable anger
So she dropped in a man's pocket
A carefully-lit rocket
And down his trousers she stuck a live banger.

I think we'd better get this one locked, don't you . . . .

*The* **Banshee** *jumps out.*

**Banshee**
There was a young woman named Page
Who spent most of her life in a rage
The solution, they thought
Was to send her to court
And put Page, in a rage, in a cage!

*As she reels off her limericks, she gives them to people.*

There was a girl called Cecilia Morse
Who got attacked on the street of course
When hassled and baited
She retaliated
Now she's banged up and feeling remorse!

**Bailey Two** I wonder if we could just herd her back into the . . .

**Banshee**
There was a young woman called Hicks
Was put in a cell 'cos she nicks
Asked why, she said 'honey
I do it for money
And darling, occasionally, for kicks'!

**Bailey Two** Girlie, if you go round that way . . and I . .

**Banshee**
There was a young woman called Read
Who stole out of desperate need
The reason she did
Was to feed her poor kid
They locked her up for this terrible deed!

**Bailey Two** We've got a nasty outbreak of poetry going on
here . . .

**Banshee**
I'm designing a new women's clink
It's innovative, what do you think?
It's *trés élégante*
And you leave when you want
And the bars are where you can drink.

**Bailey Two** Aha! The way to deal with these women is to know
how to talk to them! (*Confidentially.*) . . . You see . . . a lot of these
women write . .

**Banshee** (*also confidentially*)
It's another way to fight
As things get worse
I write it in verse
At night in the twenty-four hour light!

**Bailey Two** (*confidentially*) . . . it's a way of getting out their
frustrations . .

**Banshee**
Another way is wrecking police stations
But your knuckles, it's true
All turn black and blue
And the filth tend to lose patience!

**Bailey Two** (*to* **Banshee**) . . . That's some lovely poetry you've
penned

**Banshee**
Yes, I write them for many a friend
But here's one for you

Now here's what you do
Just stick it right up your rear end!

**Bailey Two** Now, don't you take that tone with me!

**Banshee**
I won't, if you'd just let me free
But I can't feel much love
For the fist in the glove
Of the hand who is turning the key.

**Bailey Two** Well  . . if you've committed a crime

**Banshee**
Then I've got to do the time?
This man has the brain
Of a blocked-up drain
And he thinks he's a regular Einstein!

**Bailey Two** Well, don't you think I am right?

**Banshee** No, I think you're a dumb little shite!

**Bailey Two** Well at least I'm no crim!

**Banshee**
Well, listen to him
A pure soul all shining and white!
Have you never done anything shady?

**Bailey Two** No . . .

**Banshee** Always taken 'no' from a lady?

**Bailey Two** Well . .

**Banshee** Never taken what's not yours?

**Bailey Two** Ah . . .

**Banshee** Never lifted from stores?

**Bailey Two** Hardly eve . . .

**Banshee** Never driven under the influence of drink?

**Bailey Two** Lady and shady doesn't rhyme with 'drink'

**Banshee**
Who gives a stuff what you think?
Never dropped litter on the street?

**Bailey Two** Oh . . .

**Banshee** Cheated your tax . . was that sweet?

**Bailey Two** Yes!! No!!!

**Banshee**
Never got in a brawl
About nothing at all
And gone in with the fists and the feet?

**Bailey Two** Well . . some of these things, yes, so what?

**Banshee** That's what most of us are in for, you clot!

**Bailey Two** Crime must be punished

**Banshee**
It's true
As long as it isn't you!

**Bailey Two** Society has got to be protected . .

**Banshee** Get those girls in and get them injected!

**Bailey Two** There's got to be some sort of law . .

**Banshee** How about one that is fair to the poor?

**Bailey Two** I'm getting a bit of a head . . . .

**Banshee** I hope it was something I said!

**Bailey Two** It's really beginning to throb . . .

**Banshee** Try Largactyl, that'll do the job!

**Bailey Two**
It's getting worse, getting worse
Do we have to do everything in verse???

**Banshee** (*shouting*)
The reason I do things in rhyme
Is to make some sense of my time!

In chaos and disaster
Rhyme works like a plaster
Keeps my wound free of dirt and grime!!

**Bailey Two** (*shouting*)
I really can't take any more poetry
It's beginning to threaten my sanity
Oh look . . I've caught it now
You're contagious you cow
I'll have to go into psychiatry!!!

**Bailey Two**
Please . . . I beg you . . one time
Say something that doesn't rhyme!!!

**Banshee** Yes. Something that doesn't rhyme. Okay.


Scene Five

**The Knife Act**

**Banshee**
The curtains were stiff with suspense
The audience quiet as death
Everyone's throat was dry
Everyone held their breath
Everyone's heart beat fast
Everyone grinned like a clown
They had all come to see
The hottest act in town . . .

**Bailey Two** This rhymes . . . .

**Banshee**
Somewhere an orchestra played
A cascade of glittering chords
Suddenly a choir sang
With words like slashing swords
A woman stepped onto the stage
And bowed her neck modestly down

This is what they had come to see
The hottest act in town . . .

She was wearing high stilettos
And was somewhat scantily dressed
She wore a spangled bikini
Where I'd have worn my vest
She stood there breathing evenly
Her breast rose up and down
And she was ready to perform
The hottest act in town . . .

**Bailey Two** This still rhymes . . . it does . . .

**Banshee**
From a stand she took some knives
She held them up one by one
They were sharp, they were long and thin
Like tiaras they glittered and shone
She held them by their points
They circled around and around
As she threw them at herself
The hottest act in town . . . .

She didn't have far to throw them
So every one found its target
This was the act that had thrilled them
From Scarborough to Margate
This was what they had come to see
A woman pinning herself down
Stabbing herself with daggers
The hottest act in town . . .

**Bailey Two** This rhymes.

**Banshee** No, it doesn't. Not really.

After the knives she crossed the stage
And we thought, she's taking a rest
But she took a wine glass, broke it
And stuck the jagged edge in her chest

She cried 'Isn't this original?
I perform this up and down
I learned these tricks in prison
For the hottest act in town . . .'

**Bailey Two** Oh . . now . . . this is getting a bit too soap-box for me . . . Girlie . . .

**Girlie** *and* **Bailey Two** *start circling* **Banshee**.

**Banshee**
She banged her head on the floor
And then again on the floor

**Banshee** *does too*.

Crying 'What about this then?'
And then on a handy door

*She does*.

Then she found a two-inch nail . . .

**Bailey Two** Girlie . . get her!

**Banshee**
And crying 'here's a trick I've found
I take my eye out so I can't see
I'm the hottest act in town!!'

**Girlie** *has caught her*.

**Bailey Two** Hold her!

**Girlie** *does*.

Put her back.

**Girlie** *starts to*.

You see . . . they're a danger to themselves!

**Girlie** *frog-marches* **Banshee** *back*.

**Banshee** (*to* **Girlie**)
Here's one for you . . .
There was a young woman named woman
Whose job was locking up women
When asked why she did
Said 'I do as I'm told
I'm a woman who locks up, for men, women!'

Doesn't rhyme at all, does it?

*Door closes.* **Girlie** *looks at her keys.*

**Bailey Two** and lock . . .

**Girlie** *locks the door.*

Yes. I should just think so too! Well . . . that was a nasty
outbreak of poetry there . . . I'm metaphysically exhausted . .
Girlie . . . I think I'll go get a spiritual pick-me-up. (*He goes off
and returns immediately with a glass of whiskey.*) There we are.
(*Drinks.*)

*From offstage we hear the* **Screws Sisters***:* **Sue, Lou** *and* **Moo.**

**Sue** Doo!

**Lou** Doo!

**Moo** Doo!

**Bailey Two** What was that?

**Sue** Doo!

**Lou** Doo!

**Moo** Doo!

**Bailey Two** Sounds like . . notes! Sounds like . . musical notes!

**Sue** Doo!

**Lou** Doo!

**Moo** Doo!

**Bailey Two** Sounds like . . close harmony! Sounds like a nasty outbreak of close harmony singing! (*Exits*.)

(*Offstage*.) What are you doing?

**Screws Sisters** Doo!

**Bailey Two** What are you in costume now for?

**Screws Sisters** Doo!

**Bailey Two** You're not on till the second act!

**Screws Sisters** Doo!

**Bailey Two** I'm very disappointed!

**Screws Sisters** Doo!

**Bailey Two** I thought I could rely on you to pull together as a team!

**Screws Sisters** Doo!

**Bailey Two** I've got an audience warmed up out there . . I've got to leave them to come and sort you lot out . . . oh my God . . . I've got an audience out there!!! . . and nothing's happening!!! Get out, get out . . go on . . . get yourselves on!!! Honestly . . . from now on . . . I'm working with animals . . I tell you . . . more bloody reliable!!!


Scene Six

**The Screws Sisters**

**Sue** Doooh!

**Lou** Doooh!

**Moo** Doooh!

**Sue** Hellooo!

**Lou** Hellooo!

**Moo** Hellooo!

**Sue** I'm Sue!

**Lou** I'm Lou!

**Moo** I'm Moo!

**Screws Sisters** We are the . . . Screws Sisters!!!

*They come on. They are a cross between prison officers and the Andrews Sisters. They sing the following, close harmony, exquisite song, with relevant routine: dance steps and movement.*

*Song: Keys*

We like doing it with keys
Somehow it gets us in the knees
When we rattle them, oh please
Just forget the birds and bees!
Teach me about those locks and keys!
We like doing it with keys!

It makes us itch like we've got fleas
When we're dressed up in our keys
Those girls all think we're such a tease
When we rattle them, they freeze
We say 'What's up, got some disease?'

We've got them banged up with our keys
We use them with such expertise
We bark just like some Pekinese
When we think about our keys
We like doing it with keys

And when we think about a lock
We get wound up like a clock
We watch them standing in the dock
And then we go tick-tock
And all our jewellery we'd hock

And our knees they start to knock
And then we really start to rock
And then we're crowing like a cock
Because we have them under lock
Yeah, under lock and key . .

I'm buzzing like a bee
I'm bending like a tree
I'm surging like the sea
Because we stop them being free

With just a lock and key
We like doing it with keys
Got serious knocking in the knees
Rock roll
Lock hole
Oh please!

We like doing it with keys!

**Sue** I joined the prison service because I wanted to help women.

**Lou** I joined the prison service because I wanted a job.

**Moo** I joined the prison service because I wanted to boss someone around.

**Sue** I joined the prison service because I believe in God.

**Lou** I joined the prison service because I believe in money.

**Moo** I joined the prison service because I believe in pain.

**Sue** I actually always wanted to be a social worker.

**Lou** I actually wanted to be an army officer.

**Moo** I actually wanted to be a German Shepherd dog.

**Sue** I see the women in here as pathetic, sad, miserable failures of our social system.

**Lou** I see the women in here as squaddies in the army of life.

**Moo** I see the women in here as little as possible.

**Sue** I think of them as girls. Little girls.

**Lou** I think of them as material. Raw material.

**Moo** I think of them as game. Fair game.

**Sue** I'm not racist. Not at all. I have a great affinity with all the ethnic minorities.

**Lou** I'm not racist. Not at all. Are they different colours? They all look grey to me.

**Moo** I'm not racist. Not at all. I hate every one of them.

**Sue** I see the women in here as . . . disadvantaged.

**Lou** Disturbed.

**Moo** Disgusting.

**Sue** Disorientated.

**Lou** Disobedient.

**Moo** Dismembered!

**Sue** Disabled . . .

**Lou** Disrespectful . .

**Moo** Disembowelled.

**Sue** The main rewards of being in the prison service are feeling that you are helping these people to rehabilitate themselves into society . . .

**Lou** The main rewards of being in the prison service are feeling that you are helping these people to distinguish between right and wrong . . .

**Moo** The main rewards of being in the prison service are feeling that you are helping yourself to these people's tea, sugar, tobacco, coffee, towels, sheets . . .

**Sue** It's like being . . . in Church.

**Lou** It's like being . . . in The Forces . .

**Moo** It's like being . . . in THE GRAVY! (*Sings.*) Dooooh!

**Sue** (*sings*) Dooooh!

**Lou** (*sings*) Dooooh!

**Sue** (*sings*) Sue!

**Lou** (*sings*) Lou!

**Moo** (*sings*) Moo!

**Screws Sisters**
We just like doing it with keys
Somehow it gets us in the knees
When we rattle them, oh please!
Just forget the birds and bees!
Teach us about those locks and keys
We like doing it with keys!

**Sue** *and* **Lou** *dance off.*

**Moo**
I'm buzzing like a bee
I'm bending like a tree
I'm surging like the sea
Because we stop them being free!!

*She goes ape shit: A wild frenzied dance.*

*At the height of* **Moo**'*s frenzy,* **Sue**'*s voice from behind the cases.*

**Sue** Oh, Moooo  . . ooh!

**Moo** *stops. Realises where she is, walks off with great dignity.*


Scene Seven

**Cardboard Boxes**

*Street noises. From behind the cases we hear mutterings and whisperings.*

**Tina** Psssst!

**Kim** Psssst!

**Tina** Psssst! Psssst!

**Kim** Pssssst! Psssst! . . . . . psssst . . .

**Tina** Pssssst . . . Kim . . . is that you?

**Kim** Yeah . . . . Tina . . is that you?

**Tina** Yeah . . s'me. Where're you?

**Kim** M'ere Teen . . .

**Tina** Walk towards my voice . . .

**Kim** I'll walk towards yer smell . .

**Tina** Shurrup!

**Kim** You shurrup, smelly!

**Tina** Smelly yerself!

*From each side of the cases come two figures . . .* **Kim** *and* **Tina**. *They are teenage girls. They meet each other.*

**Kim** Hiya, Smelly!

**Tina** Hiya, Smelly!

*They laugh and hit each other in a friendly fashion.*

*Suddenly they are brightly lit and a nice concerned middle-class voice addresses us . . .*

**Interviewer** Kim is fifteen, Tina is sixteen and three-quarters. They are both homeless.

**Tina** Well . . . yeah . . . what we do all day is sit here. When it's fine weather.

**Interviewer** What do you do when it's raining?

**Tina** We stand.

**Kim** (*in mid-speech*) . . naw . . I left school cos it di'ant do the subjects I needed . . .

**Interviewer** Like what?

**Kim** Architecture . . . building construction . . martial arts . . . self defence. They just done computers and careers advice.

**Interviewer** Have you ever been in trouble with the police?

**Kim** I 'aven't. She 'as.

**Interviewer** What happened?

**Tina** Well . . . I borrowed this crane, right . . off of a building site . . . and I drove it down Tesco's . . . and I manœuvred the big hook under Tesco's guttering . . . then I pulled this lever marked 'LIFT' and then I lifted Tesco's three inches off of the ground. And they done me for shoplifting.

**Tina** *and* **Kim** *fall about. They stop. Look blank.*

**Interviewer** Don't you think you're rather apathetic? (*Pause.*) Do you know what that word means?

**Kim** No, and we don't care neither.

**Tina** No. (*From under her coat she produces a dog.*) This is my dog. Jason.

**Kim** I 'ad a dog an all.

**Interviewer** What happened to it?

**Kim** We ate it.

**Interviewer** You ate it?

**Kim** Well, MacDonalds was closed. And anyway, we think vegetarians are cissy.

**Tina** Yeah. This is what me and Jase do. (*She puts Jason down. Mimes.*) Could you spare 10p please . . I'm hungry . . . They go passing by . . I'm starving Mister . . do you 'ave any spare? . . . They go passing by . . I 'aven't eaten for four days . . could ya? Straight past . . . Excuse me, my dog 'asn't had any meat since . . shower of silver coins, right!!???!!!

**Interviewer** Do you have any interests?

**Kim** We like reading.

**Tina** We read Terry.

**Interviewer** Is that a magazine?

*Both stare. Then fall about. A seventeen-year-old punk lad covered in tattoos walks in.*

**Tina** This is Terry.

**Terry** I like reading. Only I only like reading books backwards. I like romantic fiction okay . . cos they're always about happy couples who split up and have finally never met each other. And I like reading the Bible backwards because then it ends up in total darkness and in the end there was Nuffink!!! My favourite tho', is this book about a zoo . . . and finally this aardvark escapes from it . .

**Kim** Wass it called?

**Terry** Unabridged Dictionary.

**Kim** Oh. Yeah.

**Tina** We don't like music but we like intimidating pop stars. We stand outside their houses and stare at their front doors. (*To* **Kim**.) Show em your bit of Luke Bros's ear.

**Kim** *does*.

I 'ad one of Rick Astley's toe-nails but I swapped it for some ripped jeans.

**Terry** I do busking, okay? And because I play to all kinds of music-loving clientele I do mos'ly speciality Ole-Tyme stuff. This is one for hay fever sufferers . . (*Sings*.) 'Don't throw bouquets at me . . '

*All three fall about.*

And this is one for traffic wardens . . (*Sings*.) 'Some day I'll fine you . . . '

*Fall about.*

And this is one for women whose men hardly evva sa'isfy 'em sexually . . (*Sings*.) 'Once in Royal David's city!  . . '

*Fall about.*

**Interviewer** What do you do when you need money?

**Tina** We sell our bodies.

**Kim** Yeah.

**Interviewer** And then what?

**Tina** With the money we get from that, we buy 'em back again.

**Kim** And then we sell 'em again. And so on.

**Tina** It's called budgeting. We saw it on *The Money Programme*.

**Terry** *goes off.*

**Interviewer** Do you encounter much child abuse?

**Kim** No, they don't always abuse you. Some of them don't use any swear words at all.

**Terry** *returns with a large cardboard box.*

**Terry** This is where I live right?

**Interviewer** In a cardboard box?

**Terry** Yeah.

**Interviewer** Why don't you live with your parents, Terry?

**Terry** Well, because they live in a cardboard box an' all. Anyway, it's in Macclesfield.

**Interviewer** Do you have any ambitions, Terry?

**Terry** (*thinks*) Yeah. I'd like to be a guardian angel.

**Interviewer** A Guardian Angel . . what . . wear a red beret and defend innocent old ladies on the tube?

**Terry** Naah! . . a proper guardian angel . . one of those with plumage what sitteth on the right hand of that geezer what says 'Suffer little children and teenagers to come unto me and I will create waterproof cardboard boxes!'

**Interviewer** Jesus!

**Terry** Oh, that's 'is name.

**Kim** We're quite interested in religion cos if you're religious you get to sleep in a 'ostal.

**Tina** And you've got to eat fruit and muesli.

**Kim** But you 'ave to shave your 'ead.

**Interviewer** And you prefer to look feminine and attractive?

**Tina** Oh, I di'ant mind . . . but it made Jason look stupid . . di'ant it Jase?

**Kim** *goes off and gets another cardboard box.*

**Kim** This is the gels' dormitory and thass the boys' dormitory . .

**Tina** (*with more boxes*) And this is the dog-kennel . .

**Terry** And this is the guest room . .

**Tina** Because Terry's Mum and Dad are coming down from Macclesfield because Terry's Mum wants a new coat and you only get camel 'air up there . . .

**Terry** What we really want to do is get Equity Cards. Then when you appear on telly they've got to pay you.

**Tina** S'right.

**Kim** 'Cos we di'ant get nuffink for *Panorama* . . .

**Tina** Or *Weld in Action*

**Terry** Or *Disaffected Youth: Crisis Special*.

**Kim** Or NUJ cards . . 'cos we di'ant get nuffink from the *Guardian* did we?

**Tina** No. The *Sun* was going to pay us . . but in the end they juss made it up, di'ant they?

**Terry** A few Members of Parliament paid me . . .

**Tina** Yeah . . . but that was *not to tell* . . . . . .

**Terry** Oh, right . . .

**Tina** Anyway . . . we gotta get in our boxes na . . .

**Terry** Get a bit of kip. Hard day tomorrer.

**Tina** Beggin'.

**Terry** Buskin'.

**Tina** Hangin' about.

**Kim** 'Ere, guy . . . there's a box ere. (*She is by the* **Zombie**'s *box*.) Wiv a' open lid. (*She flicks the lid*.) Looks drier 'n' warmer 'n' everfing than what the cardboard is . . . (*She looks in*.) Lotsa room. (*To others*.) Whyn't we go in 'ere?

**Tina** I don't like it.

**Terry** Na . . . I get that thing when you're in tight places . . .

**Kim** Claustrophobia?

**Terry** Na . . . Cramp.

**Tina** I don't like it.

**Kim** Iss gotta be warm . . iss gotta be dry . . iss gotta be betta than out on the street . .

**Tina** 'As it?

**Kim** I fink I'll give it a whirl. Comin'?

**Tina** Iss breakin' and enterin'.

**Kim** No . . iss juss enterin' . . . What can you lose?

**Tina** I dunno.

**Terry** Can I 'ave your box then? Like cavity wall insulation.

**Kim** 'Course.

**Terry** (*puts one box inside another box inside another box*) Beautiful. Fantastic. Wicked. Thass betta than a Barratt home that. Last longer too. And now a song for the young everywhere . . (*Sings.*) 'And I think to myself . . what a wonderful world . . . ' (*Exits carrying all but one of the boxes.*)

**Kim** Well. M'off then.

**Tina** 'Kay.

**Kim** 'Bye then.

**Tina** 'Bye.

**Kim** 'Bye Jason. (*To* **Tina**.) Don't do anyfing I wouldn't do.

**Tina** There isn't anyfing you wouldn't do!

**Kim** Thass true.

*They fall about. Look at each other.* **Kim** *gets in the box pulls lid half down.* **Tina** *watches.*

**Kim** Hey . . s'alright! S'dark though. There's a light here . . . What . . . Oh no . . . . No! No! No! Tina!!!!!

*The lid closes. There is silence.*

**Interviewer** Tina . . . as a young person in Great Britain today
. . . how would you describe yourself?


Scene Eight

**Girl in a Box**

*Song: Girl in a Box*

**Tina**
Born a girl
That's a box
Tied up pretty in pink
Who'd choose that as a Christening gift?
I'd rather take to drink!

Born too poor
That's a box
Tied up in old rope
Who'd choose that for a Birthday treat?
I'd rather smoke some dope!

When
I could be
Up in the sky
Flying hot-air balloons

Got no job
That's a box
Tied up in a queue
Who'd choose that for a Valentine wish?
I'd rather sniff some glue!

When
I should be
High on a cloud
Flying hot-air balloons

Got no hope
That's a box
Tied up in red tape

Who'd choose that for a Christmas gift?
I'd rather try to escape!

When
I should have
Sun on my face
Flying hot-air balloons

Got no home
It's a box
On a windy street
Who'd choose that for a rosy future?

When
I should have
Wind in my hair
Flying hot-air balloons!

**Tina** *picks up her box. Exits.* **Kim** *is left onstage in her box.*


Scene Nine

**Earth**

*As* **Tina** *exits one way,* **Bailey Three** *played by yet another actor, comes on the other way.*

**Bailey Three** Well . . . I thought I heard a sound . . but I couldn't find a dickie bird . . hope it wasn't all very *flat* without me! Must've been, without a *man* to keep things moving! Eh, Girlie? (*Points to another door.*) Let's see what little surprise we've got in store here . . .

**Girlie** *unlocks it. A face looks out, radiant with pleasure. It is* **Rosie**.

**Rosie** Oooooh! (*Her door has been unlocked.*) Aaaaaah! (*It pushes open.*) Eeeeeeeh! (*She walks out. She is wearing gumboots.*) Ouuuuuuuh! (*She catches sight of the audience.*) Mmmmmmmmmh! (*She catches sight of* **Bailey Three**.) Hmmmmmmm . . . (*She goes back and comes out with a spade.*) Aaaaaah!!!! *Finally* . . . when I gave up screaming and fighting and banging my head on everything *solid*, they put me in THE GARDEN!!! Gave me some wellies! And

. . . a spade! I was in . . . the OPEN AIR!!!!! And things . . .
were GREEN!!!! And SKY!!!!!! And FRESH SMELLS!!!!!! I
thought my knickers would never dry!!!! I knelt down and picked
a leaf and put it in my mouth and it was MINT!!! It was the
BEST thing I'd ever, EVER . . tasted. My plan was to dig an
escape tunnel. Figured if I dug down 15 foot then along 75 foot
then up 15 foot, I'd come up in the pub beer garden across from
prison. Figured if I stayed on gardens I'd be having a pint in that
pub in four months, thirteen days. I started digging on a likely
spot. I was just starting on the top soil when a voice from a
window yelled 'Stop!!!!' That's the end of the escape-tunnel plan,
I thought. But the voice said, 'Don't dig *there*, that's Ruth Ellis's
grave.' I said 'Who's Ruth Ellis then?' And the voice said, 'She
was the last woman to be hanged in England! Dig somewhere
else!' And I thought . . . I'm standing with the edge of my spade
in the last woman to be hanged in England! And it done
something to my head it was like somebody had put a spade in
the top of my brain and lifted off the top soil and there, lying in
the earth were all these dead women! It was like I was on one of
those archeological digs, where you find old brooches and knives
and bottles and nutshells, only I was finding these dead women!
And I thought about that place . . Pompeii . . . where that
volcano erupted and all the lava just covered everything and
everybody was stuck doing what they was doing that day, and I
thought, suppose that happened here, this prison suddenly gets
swamped with lava and hundreds of years later somebody like
me is digging and finds this prison and all these women stuck
doing what they was doing that day, what would the person
digging think? I tried to get my head round that. They'd find this
building full, full of women. 'What's this all about then.' That's
what the archeologist would say. A building full of women. Why
did these women live all together? Were they some sort of holy
order? Was it . . a brothel? Was it a place where women could go
and enjoy each other's company? They all seem to be in together,
in these small rooms. Then, when they swept away some of the
dust, they'd find that some of these women wore the same clothes
and had these belts with these metal objects on them. Was that a
type of jewellery, wonders the archeologist. And then the
archeologist says 'Wait a minute . . this is a key!!!' All these

women in the same clothes have got all these keys . . and the
women in the same clothes are all outside the rooms with the
other women inside. And the archeologist suddenly puts it all
together . . . 'Sussed it!' she says, 'The women in this place must
be very, very important in some way, very, very special with very
mighty powers because why else would they be so carefully
watched over and kept safe?' And the archeologist thinks she has
discovered the truth about this society. Its Women have such
Mighty Power! I come out of my head because someone is
saying: 'Rosie . . you turned over that flower bed yet?' And I'm
back in the prison garden, next to Ruth Ellis's grave. But I'm not
really back. My head's been turned over. Instead of seeing the
usual gloom and grey, I see mighty power. No wonder they've
got us under lock, we're mighty! No wonder they've got us under
the thumb, we're powerful! No wonder they've got us on tranqs,
our heads are full of danger to them! And instead of the escape
tunnel to the pub across the road, I'm digging a new tunnel. It's
through all this shit they shovelled into my head, mud to stop me
moving, cement to keep me still, dirt to muck me up and I'm
sowing seeds everywhere. 'You think you're dirt, but you're not
kid' I say to one. 'You're the plant, not the fertiliser' I say to
another 'Don't dig out . . . dig IN!' I say. You're a lovely Rose.
You're a scent of summer. You're a whole bouquet. You're a
fucking wonderful flower garden!! (*She smiles.*) And you know
how long it took me to think through all that? Three hours.
That's the time it took to plant flowers all around Ruth Ellis's
grave.


Scene Ten

**The Strong Woman Act**

**Bailey Three** (*claps*) Fine words.

**Rosie** *says nothing.*

Nice concept.

**Rosie** *says nothing.*

Very neat tying up of metaphysical and philosophical conceits.

**Rosie** *looks mild.*

Don't you think?

**Rosie** *looks mild.*

Wouldn't you agree?

**Rosie** *says nothing.*

Eh?

**Rosie** *says nothing.*

Mmm?

**Rosie** *says nothing.*

Why don't you answer me?

**Rosie** *looks.*

Cat got your tongue?

**Rosie** *looks.*

Lost for words?

**Rosie** *looks.*

Well . . . I don't call this much of an act!

**Rosie** *says nothing.*

Not very entertaining!

**Rosie** *says nothing.*

I've had more fun in a cat litter tray!

**Rosie** *says nothing.*

I've been more amused cutting my toenails!

**Rosie** *says nothing but regards him with interest.*

I've had more laughs at the dole office!

*Still nothing.*

What's wrong with you?

*Nothing.*

What's your problem?

*Nothing.*

What's the story here?

*Nothing.*

You're being very difficult! I'm getting very annoyed here! You're winding me up! Don't give me a hard time, now! You're getting me wired up, you know! You're going to make me blow my top you know if you don't watch out, I mean I'm getting very very tense here now!!!!!!

**Rosie** *has been watching him wind himself up.*

**Rosie** What do you want me to do?

**Bailey Three** Anything!!!

**Rosie** Anything? What . . . give a wolf whistle? Make a dirty telephone call? Rape somebody on a train? What?

**Bailey Three** Naw . . . don't give me that . . .

**Rosie** What? Invent the corset? Design the high-heeled shoe? Manufacture some crotchless knickers? What?

**Bailey Three** What's all this . . .

**Rosie** What? Fire a gun? Pull the pin out of a grenade? Invent a nuclear bomb? What?

**Bailey Three** Don't get clever with me!

**Rosie** Don't get clever with you? I couldn't get clever with you! That's what you *don't* want. So work out what you *do* want! What?

**Bailey Three** I just want . . .

**Rosie** Yes.

**Bailey Three** I just want . . .

**Rosie** Yes . . .

**Bailey Three** I just want . . . I'm a showman! I just want a bloody GOOD ACT!!!

**Rosie** Drum roll. (*There is a drum roll.*) What a man wants. A bloody good act. Ladies and gentlemen . . . Giving the showman what he wants . . Astounding Acts of Amazement! Shimmering Shows of Skill! Stunning Scenarios of Strength! Ladies And Gentlemen . . . The Strong Woman Act.

**Bailey Three** Ah.

**Rosie** Give the public what he wants. (*She takes him by the shoulders.*)

**Bailey Three** Well . . I didn't quite have this in mind . .

**Rosie** Astounding Acts of Amazement. (*She bends him over.*) Shimmering Shows of Skill. (*She picks him up.*) Stunning Scenarios of Strength. (*She lifts him higher.*) Ladies and Gentlemen . . . The Strong Woman Act! (*She lifts him high above her head.*)

**Bailey Three** No . . . this isn't what I had in mind at all!!! Waaaagh!

**Rosie** No . . . what you want is a strong woman you don't see! What you want is a strong woman who listens and watches and admires and bills and coos and pats and strokes and applauds and cooks and does and does and does and does for you . . . and I'll tell you something . . hard as this act is . . . it's not nearly so bloody tiring as the one you want!!!!

**Bailey Three** Can you put me down now?

*Nothing from* **Rosie**.

I mean I take your point but I have a little vertigo problem . . .

*Nothing from* **Rosie**.

Will you just bloody well put me DOWN!!!!! Girlie . . . would you just come and tickle this woman's armpits . . . aagh . . no . . . Get a ladder or something . . . Oh, thank goodness . .

**Rosie** *lets him down. He stands up. Straightens himself up.*

Right! Right! Right! (*To* **Girlie**.) *You are Fired!!!* (*To* **Rosie**.)
YOU . . . .

**Rosie** Yes.

**Bailey Three** You . . . are . . . very strong!!!

**Rosie** Yes. Watch.

**Bailey Three** Oh no . . . now what?

**Rosie** The Strong Woman Act. Astounding Acts of Amazement.
(*She takes hold of the lock on the* **Banshee**'*s case and crumbles it to
pieces*.) She uses her strength to free others.

*The lid lifts, the* **Banshee** *looks out, sees* **Rosie**.

Then she wanders off into the unrecorded mists of woman's
achievement!!!

**Rosie** *walks off and as she does* . . .

**Banshee**
There was many a woman with no name
Who did good, but received no fame
No government applauds
No history records
Ah, isn't it always the same?

**Rosie** *listens, smiles at* **Banshee** *and exits*.

**Bailey Three** (*to* **Girlie**, *with emphasis*) Get Her Back! (**Girlie**
*sits*.) Put That Dangerous Piece Of Business Back Under Lock
And Key!!!

**Bailey Three** What's Wrong With You? You Deaf?

**Banshee**
Not deaf, but discharged I fear
Oh goodness, look what I've got here!

*She brings out a large saw.*

I'll show you a trick

*To* **Girlie**.

If you'd just be a brick
And fetch me a box in, my dear!

**Girlie** *goes off.*

**Bailey Three** Don't leave me alone with this maniac!!!

**Banshee**
You've seen women sawn in half
And have to admit, it's a laugh
Would you now like to see
A man sawed in three?
What fun writing his epitaph!

**Girlie** *returns with a large, man-sized box.*

**Bailey Three** (*to the audience*) Is there a member of the police force in the audience?

**Banshee** My lovely assistant will now put this willing volunteer in this decorative box!

**Girlie** *leads* **Bailey Three** *to the box, gently but firmly.*

**Bailey Three** Don't come crying to me for your job back when this is all over! There are plenty of young women out there ready willing and able to take your place!

*He is put in the box.*

**Banshee** Now, are you feeling comfortable? Then we'll begin!!!

**Bailey Three** How come you're not speaking in rhyme any more?

**Banshee** Well, you see . . . I swapped courses . . . stopped doing the Creative Writing . . . and took up The Beginners Course in Illusion And Magic!

**Bailey Three** BEGINNERS COURSE???????

**Banshee** Yes . . . *isn't* it exciting?

**Bailey Three** Oh My God!

**Banshee** Now ladies and gentlemen . . . this is a very complex and dangerous trick for a beginner to attempt . . . so I need absolute silence! (*Waits for absolute silence.*) Now, I will be sawing the gentlemen at his kneecaps here and his neck here . . . separating him . . . then putting him back together in one piece. I think that's what our tutor said . . here goes . . fingers crossed. Oh no, can't saw with fingers crossed!

**Bailey Three** If there's a member of the audience with one shred of human decency . . .

**Banshee** Shhh . . . or you'll get me sawing all jagged!!!

**Bailey Three** Gulp!!!!

**Banshee** Now . . . . the knee thigh separation. (*She saws.*) And then . . . the head neck separation. (*She saws.*) There. Now what? (*She goes to her case, takes out an instruction sheet. Reads.*) . . saw . . . saw . . yes . . . mmm . . . 'Show the audience that the man is now in three distinct and separate pieces' . . . Right. Ladies And Gentlemen . . . Note how the man is now in three distinct and separate pieces! (*She separates the three sections, checks manual, reads.*) 'Reassemble the willing volunteer and amaze and stun your audience' . . I will now amaze and stun you, Ladies and Gentlemen, by reassembling my willing volunteer! (*She reassembles the box.*) There. (*Looks at manual.*) 'Let him out of the box' . . Ooh! (*Opens the box,* **Evvie** *lies there.*)

**Banshee** What the bloody hell are you doing there?

**Evvie** Hello!

**Banshee** Hello?

**Evvie** Hello!

**Banshee** Don't hello me . . . tell me what you're doing there!

**Evvie** It's a box. Naughty girls get put in boxes! Hello!

**Banshee** Where's the man that I left in there?

**Evvie** Man?

**Banshee** Yes, Man, dummy! Shiny suit, slicked back quiff, flares
. . man!

**Evvie** Bailey!

**Banshee** Bailey!

**Evvie** He tells me what to do.

**Banshee** Did he tell you to get in this box? Did he say where he
was going? Did you notice whether he was in three pieces or one?

**Evvie** He tells me what to do.

**Banshee** What are you . . an answerphone tape? Get up and
help me look for him. This is dreadful . . . I won't get my Illusion
and Magic Diploma!

**Evvie** He gets me up. He tells me what to do.

**Banshee** Well, he's not here, is he??? So now I'm telling you
what to do!!! Get up and help me!

**Evvie** On my own?

**Banshee** Of course on your own, dummy! What are you, a
dummy?

**Evvie** Yes.

**Banshee** Oh for goodness sake! (*She pinches* **Evvie**.)

**Evvie** Ouch!!!!

**Banshee** Hurt does it?

**Evvie** Yes . . .

**Banshee** Dummies don't hurt. You're not a dummy. Now get
up.

**Evvie** *stands up*.

See! Brilliant. A small step for woman . . . A mighty leap for the
ventriloquy business. Now, where's that wretched willing
volunteer?

*The two of them start looking around.*

**Evvie** Not in here.

**Banshee** Not in here. Honestly, this is a disastrous start for me in The Illusion and Magic World, I tell you!

**Evvie** Not in here.

**Banshee** Not here. I bet David Nixon didn't kick off his career like this!

**Evvie** Maybe he's in one of the locked cases?

**Banshee** Good thinking, dummy. (*To* **Girlie**.) Lend us your keys, would you dearie?

**Evvie** My name's Evvie. Not dummy.

**Banshee** Evvie. Okay. Sorry. Keys, dearie.

**Evvie** What's your name?

**Banshee** I am known as 'The Banshee'!!! Poetess, Firebrand and Magic Illusionist! (*Pause, embarrassed.*) But my name's . . . Barbara.

**Evvie** Barbara. There's a pair of legs in shiny trousers in here, Barbara.

**Banshee** Oh my Goodness! Attached to anything above the knees, are they . . . . Evvie?

**Evvie** No Barbara.

**Banshee** Oh misery.

*They both search frantically through the closed cases. The three of them unlock all the cases.*

**Evvie** Barbara . . . there's a man in here in a shiny suit jacket.

**Banshee** A *whole* man, Evvie?

**Evvie** Apart from a head and a pair of legs . .

**Both**  . . From the knees down!

**Banshee** Well . . . we're two thirds of the way there!!!

**Evvie** Barbara . . . look what I've found.

**Banshee** A head. Please God, a head!!!

**Evvie** Yes.

**Banshee** Thank you God!

**Evvie** Only . . .

**Banshee** Only what . . . what's the problem?

**Evvie** Only what . . . it's a woman's head, Barbara!

*It is the* **Zombie**.

**Banshee** Oh no! Excuse me Miss . . . have you seen a man's head around here at all?

**Zombie** (*pause*) What on earth do you want a man's head for?

*Silence.*

**Banshee** Well  . . I was doing this act right . . .

(*Pause.*)

I cut this man up in three right . . .

(*Pause.*)

and there's a bit in there . .

(*Pause.*)

and a bigger bit in there right . .

(*Pause.*)

and now we just need . . .

(*Pause, to* **Evvie**.)

What on earth do we want a man's head for?

**Evvie** I don't know Barbara.

**Banshee** I don't know either, Evvie.

**Zombie** Did it belong to a man with a big black quiff . .

**Banshee**  . . shiny suit . . .

**Zombie** . . . flares . .

**Banshee** Awful dress sense.

**Evvie** Clammy hands.

**Zombie** Kept you locked up in boxes?

**Banshee** That's the one . .

**Zombie** Just like me . . .

**Banshee** Oh, I'm sorry . . let us . . . .

**Banshee** *and* **Evvie** *help* **Zombie** *out of her prison.*

**Zombie** Very nice. You sawed a man into three . . . And he vanished?

**Banshee** Yes.

**Zombie** Nice trick.

**Banshee** Yes!

**Zombie** And these are your assistants . . . who opened all these locks?

**Banshee** Yes.

**Zombie** Nice job.

**Evvie** Yes. My name's Evvie, this is Barbara, this is . . .

**Girlie** Jane.

**Evvie** This is Jane.

**Zombie** They call me The Zombie. My name's Patricia Letitia Lily May! Can you believe it? (*She roars with laughter. All laugh.*) What was his name?

**Banshee** Bailey.

**Evvie** Old Bailey.

*They roar again.*

**Zombie** He was a trial, wasn't he?

*They roar again.*

**Banshee** What a case!

*Off they go again.*

**Evvie** Ooh!

**Banshee** What is it?

**Evvie** I've got a pain in my chest!

**Zombie** Like what?

**Evvie** Like . . . like I want to sing . . .

**Banshee** Well . . sing.

*Song: She*

**Evvie**
I've been confined
I've been fined
I've been undermined
But I'm me
I've been blind
I've mainlined
Gone out of my mind
But I'm me
I'm still SHE

**Banshee**
I've done crime
I've done time
Done the prison pantomime
But I'm me
I've been nicked
I've been tricked
Been viciously kicked
But I'm me
I'm still SHE

**Zombie**
I've been short of dosh
Been talked at posh
Eaten prison nosh
Had the liquid cosh
But I'm me
I've lashed out
Splashed out
Been laid out
Knocked out
Locked out

Been full of doubt
But I'm me
I'm still SHE

**All**
I've been through screws, abuse
Misuse, had the blues
Sniffed glues
Blown my fuse
Appeared on the news
Been through isolation
Deprivation
Self-mutilation
Rehabilitation
But I'm me
I've been through strip-searches
Churches
In depth researches
Investigated
Incarcerated
Hated, gated
Retaliated
But I'm me
I'm still SHE

I've been off the wall
In Bulwood Hall
Been very strange
In Askham Grange
Known tears and blood
In Cookham Wood
Risley was grisly
And Styal was a pile
Fell off my perch
In Pucklechurch
Muppet on a string
In Durham Women's Wing
Got the boot in
Low Newton
Had a very long stay

In Holloway
But I'm me
I'm still SHE.


Scene Eleven

**The Big Finale**

*The music from the song continues under the following.*

**Evvie** Barbara . . . . .

*Banshee* Yes, Evvie . . . .

**Evvie** Where do you think Old Bailey is? (*She looks nervously at the cases.*) All his bits are . . . around somewhere . . . (*More nervous.*) And . . . all these cases . . . are unlocked . . .

*They all look uneasy.*

**Zombie** Oh!

**Banshee** What?

**Zombie** You know how we were in a box each?

**Banshee** Yeeeees . . .

**Zombie** Do you think . . . . there might be anybody else in there? . . . . .

**Evvie** Ooooooooooh!

**Zombie** Let's leg it!!

**Banshee** Come on then!

**Evvie** No.

**Banshee** What?

**Evvie** No. They might need help . . . And if Bailey's hanging about . . . .

*Pause.*

**Banshee** All right!!!

*They approach the cases.*

You first!

**Evvie** No you!

**Zombie** No you!

*Lots of this. Finally* **Evvie** *goes first. She enters the case which* **Tina** *left.*

**Evvie** It's very dark in here . . . I don't know which way to go . . . It's a long tunnel . . . what's down this way . . .

*Silence.*

**Banshee** Evvie? Evvie! She's disappeared. You'd better go in and look for her!

**Zombie** Why me?

**Banshee** I'm scared!

**Zombie** I'm petrified!

**Banshee/Zombie** Let's both go.

(*They enter.*)

It's very dark in here . . .
I don't know which way to go . . .
It's a long tunnel . . .
What's down this way . . . .

*Silence. As this happens,* **Kim** *appears elsewhere.*

**Kim** Hello  . . wass this music then? Tina! Terry! Where are ya? There's some finale music playing . .

**Terry** *and* **Tina** *appear.*

**Kim/Terry/Tina**
Got no hope
That's a box
Tied up in red tape
Who'd choose that for a Christmas gift
We'd rather try to escape
Got no home
It's a box
On a windy street
Who'd choose that for a rosy future?
When
We should have
Wind in our hair

**Tina** This way!

**Terry** Na . . this way . . .

**Kim** Na . . this way . . .

*This continues until.*

**Tina** Oh no . . . . where's everybody gone?

*We hear the 'dooh dooh doohs' of the* **Screws Sisters**.

Wass that noise?

*She goes off to investigate. The* **Screws Sisters** *enter.*

**Screws Sisters**
We've stopped doing it with keys
The doctor said 'it's a disease
To like doing it with keys'
She said 'You're sick', we said 'oh please
Cure us of these locks and keys'
She got some pills and said 'take these'
We took the dose and now, oh Jeez . .

We're buzzing like a bee
We're bending like a tree
We're waving like the sea
Because we like them going free . . .

**Lou** and **Sue** exit.
**Moo** stays on and does a repeat of her frenzied dance.
**Evvie**'s head appears at a gap.

**Evvie** Barbara . . . Oh . . you're not Barbara . . .

**Moo** goes off.

I've found something awful in here . . . You know we were
looking for Bailey . . well . . . I think I've found him . . .

She disappears.

One, two, then three **Baileys** appear.

They Sing

**Baileys**
Hey there, little girl
Feeling small
I'll be your pursuer
Brave strong and tall.

Hey there, little girl
Feeling weak?
I'll be your nightmare
We'll dance cheek to cheek.

Like an oil slick on a sunny beach
Like a wasp on a sticky peach
Like a bloodsucking slimy leech
I'll be
There for you
Like war when you pray for peace
Like troubles that never cease
Like a crippling brain disease
I'll be
There for you
Always there.

We're the root of the trouble
Haha you're seing double
Have you been at the tipple

Haha you're seeing triple
There's a host of us you see
Who'll stop you getting free
Where women belong is in the wrong
In the WRONG!!!

Where are my girls? Where are my freaks? Where are my examples to society? Where've they gone?

*They go on the rampage searching for the others.*

Where are my lost children? In here? I'll find you . . . I'll get you . . .

**Evvie** Barbara . . . there's a lot of men with shiny suits and quiffs crawling about in here . . .

**Bailey One** There's one of them . . . now, if I go back down here . . . I'll be able to . . .

**Banshee** I wonder if this sort of problem ever happens to Paul Daniels . . .

**Bailey Two** I want all this lot rounded up and back under lock and key . . .

**Evvie** Barbara . . . do you know any tricks for disappearing men permanently . . . .

**Bailey Three** It wasn't like this at Butlins . . . .

*The chase continues as* **Rosie** *walks in.*

**Rosie** There was once a baby girl born and she had an eye here, an eye here and an eye here, in the middle of her forehead. And she had an arm here, an arm here, an arm here and an arm here. And she had a leg here, a leg here, a leg here and a leg here. She could see further, lift more, walk longer, than anybody else. She was different. So a man came along and put her in a cage to show her off. And he charged people to see her and people came and looked and went away saying 'We've just seen a freak' and the girl who could see further, lift more, walk longer, made a sign which she hung above her in her cage. It said:

The one who cages,
The one who is caged,
The one who knows the cage is there.
Which one is the freak?

*Exit.*